D0438623

The Unbeatable Boys' Book

HOW TO BE THE ULTIMATE CHAMPION

Written by Huw Davies
Illustrated by Simon Ecob

Edited by Liz Scoggins
Designed by Angie Allison

The Unbeatable Boys' Book

HOW TO BE THE ULTIMATE CHAMPION

Buster Books

First published in Great Britain in 2009 by Buster Books,
an imprint of Michael O'Mara Books Limited,
9 Lion Yard, Tremadoc Road, London SW4 7NQ

www.mombooks.com/busterbooks

DISCLAIMER

The publisher and author disclaim all liability, as far as is legally permitted,
for any accidents or injuries or loss that may occur as a result of the use or
misuse of the information and guidance given in this book.

We urge you, at all times, to make yourself aware of, and obey, all laws,
regulations and local by-laws, and respect all rights, including the rights of
property owners. Always respect other people's privacy and remember to
ask a responsible adult for assistance and take their advice whenever
necessary. Above all, remember to exercise good common sense and take
all necessary safety precautions when preparing to attempt an activity,
particularly when using new equipment or techniques.

Text and illustrations copyright © Buster Books 2009
Cover design by Angie Allison (from an original design by www.blacksheep-uk.com)
Cover illustration by Paul Moran

The words of the 'Ka Mate' haka on pages 24 and 25 are just one variation of
a traditional song, which can be found in slightly differing versions. The version
published here can be found at www.folksong.org.nz and is widely
used in public performances of the haka.

All rights reserved. No part of this publication may be reproduced, stored in a retrieval
system, or transmitted by any means, without the prior permission in writing of the
publisher, nor be otherwise circulated in any form of binding or cover other than that in
which it is published and without a similar condition including this condition being
imposed on the subsequent purchaser.

A CIP catalogue record for this book is available from the British Library.

ISBN: 978-1-906082-69-7

2 4 6 8 10 9 7 5 3 1

Printed and bound in England by Clays Ltd, St Ives plc

Papers used by Buster Books are natural, recyclable products
made from wood grown in sustainable forests. The manufacturing processes
conform to the environmental regulations of the country of origin.

CONTENTS

CALLING ALL UNBEATABLE BOYS

Do you want to know how to become a world-record holder, how to serve an ace at tennis, or do the haka? It's all in here, but first a word of warning. You can't be unbeatable if you are injured or hurt in any way. We recommend that you take all necessary precautions to make your progress to 'unbeatability' a safe and injury-free one. Remember these key points:

• Always wear protective gear wherever necessary – especially when riding a bike or a skateboard, for example.

• Never battle through the pain of an injury – stop and rest or seek medical advice.

• Don't attempt any of the activities in this book alone, or just with friends, unless your parents or guardians say it's okay, and know exactly where you are going.

• If you or your parents have any concerns about your fitness or health before taking on an unbeatable challenge, check with your doctor first.

Finally, if any words are unfamiliar to you, you'll find that many of them are explained in the glossary on page 126.

HOW TO WIN A CAMEL RACE

Camel racing is a popular sport, particularly in the Middle East, where it has been practised for as long as horse racing. To be a camel jockey you'll need to be quite fearless, as a good racing camel can maintain a speed of about 40 kilometres per hour, and sprint at up to 65 kilometres per hour.

DON'T GET THE HUMP

Of course, you'll need to know how to get on to a camel before you race one. Fortunately, it's easier to get on to a racing camel than a wild one – they're much more used to it.

1. The handler will make the camel kneel down first, but ask him to put one foot on the camel's front leg to stop it getting up before you are ready.

2. Now place one foot in the stirrup nearest to you. Be sure that your right foot goes in the right stirrup, and your left foot goes in the left stirrup, otherwise you'll end up facing backwards and feeling very silly.

3. Swing your other leg over the saddle in one swift movement and sit back. The camel brings its rear legs up first when it stands, so lean back to avoid being thrown forwards. Then, as its front legs come up, lean forwards.

Now you're ready to race!

Riding a camel is not at all like riding a horse. The camel puts its feet down differently, which makes it sway from side to side. When this is happening at high speed, you need to have the right skills to stay aboard. Draw your knees up to your

8

chest as the camel starts moving. This will help you cope with the swaying motion. As the camel gets up to speed, stretch one leg forwards over its neck to help you get more comfortable. The very best of luck!

HOW TO START PRECISION KITING

Kite flying is an ancient tradition, thousands of years old. One of the most popular forms today is 'precision kiting', or stunt kiting, which is often done with a triangular kite, called a 'delta'. A delta kite has two lines – one held in each hand.

LAUNCHING YOUR KITE

1. First, make sure your lines are exactly equal in length. Each line should be between 20 and 30 metres long.

2. Stand with the wind behind you, and hold the handles out in front of you. Get a helper to hold the kite slightly off the ground at the full length of the lines.

3. If the wind is fairly strong, your helper can just lift the kite up in the air. If the wind is less strong, you'll need to take a step back and pull both hands down to make the kite leap into the air.

4. Once your kite is up, bring your hands back up in front of your body. To make your kite swing to the right, gently pull back your right hand – to make your kite swing to the left, gently pull back your left hand.

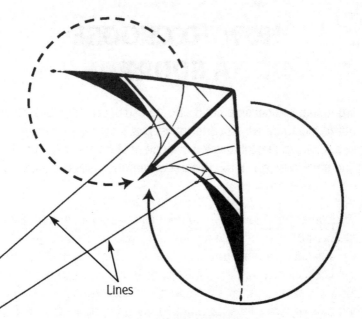

Lines

A BEGINNER'S STUNT

The figure-of-eight is a nice simple trick to start with. Here's how to do it:

1. Steer your kite to the right, then slowly switch the position of your hands, bringing your left hand back level with your right hand to straighten up. Carry on pulling your left hand back to make your kite sweep to the left.

2. Keep gently steering right, then straightening, and steering left to keep your kite sweeping in wide figures-of-eight in the sky.

Warning. Always be considerate of other people in the immediate area, as being hit on the head with a kite is very painful. Also remember that you must never fly a kite in a storm, or near any electricity lines.

HOW TO CHOOSE A SPORT

If you want to become good at a particular sport, it's best to try out as many different sports as possible before you choose just one. This way you'll develop a range of skills and strengths, and from there you'll be able to develop the skills you need for your favourite sport.

You can get an idea of where your talents might lie by looking at your parents and their family, since you share their genes. For example, perhaps your dad is a good long-distance runner, but can't sprint very fast. If it looks as though you come from a family of non-sprinters, then you may be better suited to the triathlon or marathons. Or maybe your mum and her family are all tall. If you're likely to be tall, you'll obviously have an advantage in sports like basketball. These are great clues to how you might develop and could point you towards a sport you may want to focus on when you are older.

Remember that the very best sports-people are quite unusual. They might have above-average lung size that will give them the advantage over most average people. As long as you enjoy the sports you play, you'll be doing well – you may even uncover a talent for a sport that you would otherwise have ignored, missing a chance to be good at it. While you're still growing, it's hard to know how you'll develop, so it's best not to specialize too soon. What's more, if you specialize too early, you may end up not liking your sport after a while. If you choose a sport after trying lots of them, you're more likely to want to keep playing it for the rest of your life.

HOW TO HIT A HOME RUN

In baseball, a home run is achieved when you hit the ball so hard that you can run around all four bases in one go. Hitting a home run is every young baseball player's dream. The crack of the bat on the ball, watching it soar out of the field … but you have to learn how to hit the ball first, so here's what to do:

GET THE BAT ON THE BALL

1. Hold the bat with your strong hand above your weaker hand, and with the handle of the bat gripped firmly, using your fingers as well the palms of your hands.

2. Stand side-on to the pitcher with your knees bent, and your feet a little more than shoulder-width apart to make a stable base to hit the ball from. Put slightly more weight on your back foot, so that you can step into your swing.

3. Hold the bat behind you, at about head height, ready to swing, with your arms away from your body.

4. As the pitcher throws the ball towards you, step

forwards to meet it. Keep your upper body and your head still, and make sure your eyes stay on the ball.

5. As the ball arrives, swing into it, keeping your swing level, and follow through with your bat, swinging it right around your body.

OUT OF THE PARK

Depending on the size of the field, you might need to hit the baseball well over 100 metres to get it out of the ball park – or at least far enough away from the outfielders to give you a chance at running around all four bases. What makes hitting a home run different is that you have to swing with more power and speed – that's obvious. You also have to focus on hitting the ball along the natural line of your swing, where you get most power. Try out this technique:

1. Always watching the ball as it leaves the pitcher's hand, keep the bat level, and the elbow of your weaker arm into your body. As you swing, rotate your body, and transfer your weight from your back foot to your front foot.

2. Build up the momentum in your swing as it comes around to meet the ball so that your hit has maximum power when it makes contact with the ball.

3. Swing fast and hard. Follow through as much as possible and start running as soon as you've hit the ball!

Unbeatable tip. Once you can hit the ball hard and fast, you'll get even more distance by 'undercutting' it, which means hitting the ball slightly below centre. This will propel the ball forwards and upwards with some spin, taking it high into the air, and far out of reach of the fielders.

HOW TO THROW A CURVE BALL

A curve ball is a great weapon for a baseball pitcher to have. To the batter, the ball appears to fly through the air as normal, but it moves out away from the bat at the last moment, leaving him swinging at thin air.

'STRRRIKE!'

Throwing a curve ball is all down to using the right grip, which produces topspin on the ball, and makes it curve down to the left (or to the right, if you are a left-handed thrower). Here's how to do it:

1. Squeeze the ball between your index finger and your thumb, with your third finger down at the side, keeping the ball in place. Tilt your wrist back to the left (or the right, if you are left-handed).

2. As you throw, flick your wrist down and around, as shown. The seams on the ball will catch the air, making it spin.

15

3. Follow through with your wrist and fingers. If you don't, the ball will probably 'hang' in the air and float into the path of the batter instead of curving nicely.

4. Remember that for the pitch to be a strike, the ball must still arrive in the 'strike zone', which is roughly between the batter's knee and chest.

Experiment with different speeds and spins – the ball will curve more if it is thrown more slowly. Practise your grip regularly to get the balance just right.

Unbeatable tip. Throwing a curve ball puts some stress on your wrist and elbow, so it's important to practise the technique first with a lighter ball, such as an 'Airflo' ball, or even a tennis ball. When you have been practising for a few weeks, and your wrist and elbow are stronger, move on to a real baseball.

HOW TO START
A MEXICAN WAVE

The 'Mexican wave' has been around since the 1970s, but it became famous during the 1986 football World Cup in Mexico. It looks like a giant wave flowing around the stadium, as thousands of spectators stand up with their arms in the air, then sit down, all in sequence. Unfortunately, it is practically impossible to start a Mexican wave by yourself.

Studies have shown that it takes about 30 people to start a Mexican wave. So you need to get another 29 people in the stadium on the same 'wave'-length as you. Preferably they should be sitting to your left, as waves tend to travel clockwise around a stadium. If you have enough friends and family members around you, you'll be part-way there – then it's up to your fellow spectators to co-operate and make it happen! Try offering bribes of soft drinks, popcorn or sweets to get them to join in.

HOW TO WIN A TRIATHLON

In a triathlon race you must have the stamina to swim, cycle and run over a set distance. As well as being able to do each of these sports well, the race is often won and lost in the 'transition' between sections, when you switch between disciplines in a special transition area. Transition one, or **'T1'**, is from swimming to cycling. **'T2'** is from cycling to running.

Before the race you will be given a particular spot in the transition area. To avoid losing valuable time in the race, plan your route to this spot carefully. Time can also be gained in **T1** and **T2** by practising super-speedy mounts and dismounts when transferring to and from your bike – you'll gain valuable seconds without having to swim, cycle, or run faster.

'ON YER BIKE!'

In **T1** you need to be able to get your shoes and helmet on, push your bike to the start line, mount your bike at speed and start cycling. This must all be done in the most efficient time possible, while still dripping wet from swimming.

T1 mount. The fastest way to mount your bike is to vault on to the saddle while rolling the bike along. You could put one foot on a pedal, scoot along to build up speed, and jump on. However, if you are very daring and agile, grab the handle bars and jump straight from the ground to the saddle.

T2 dismount. For the fastest dismount, swing one leg over the saddle, leaving the other foot on its pedal. While the bike is still moving, brake and jump off immediately. Place your bike on the rack in your assigned spot, get your helmet off, and start running. Don't go off too fast though – it will make you tired very quickly after your hard work on the bike. Give your legs a little time to get used to the action of running, and you'll be able to run faster later in the section, when everyone else is slowing down.

Unbeatable tip. These skills are fairly simple, but need plenty of practice, preferably on grass for a soft landing if they should go wrong.

HOW TO PUT THE BALL BETWEEN THE POSTS

In rugby, accurate goal kicking is a great skill to have for your team, and gives your coach an extra reason to select you. Even if you don't score any tries, you will add to your team's score with your impressive goal kicks.

SWEET SPOT

A rugby ball is kicked from a 'tee'. Often you'll have a plastic tee to kick from, but if not you can use the heel of your boot to dig a small tee in the ground.

1. Place the ball on the tee and tilt it slightly forwards. This means when you kick it, your foot will hit the round 'belly' of the ball, also called the 'sweet spot'. The tip of the ball must point at your target (in between the posts).

2. 'Address' the ball. This means standing next to the ball with your non-kicking foot next to it, pointing at your target, and your kicking foot just behind it.

3. From this position, move back a few paces – you don't need a long run-up – and in your mind's eye line up the ball and the posts. Imagine kicking the ball straight between them.

4. When you are ready, move towards the ball with a curved run-up, so that you arrive at the ball side-on, with the shoulder on your non-kicking side pointing towards the posts. Look only at the ball.

5. Your last step is when your non-kicking foot lands next to the ball – it should be pointing towards the posts, too.

6. Swing your kicking leg quickly straight 'through' the ball, almost as though it isn't there. Keep your head down and your eyes on the ball.

PRACTICE MAKES PERFECT

Try out this drill to get the hang of your kicking skills.

1. Stand right in front of the posts, as close as you like, and take five kicks at goal.

2. Move 10 metres to the left and take five kicks.

3. Move 10 metres to the right and take five kicks.

Take your time with each kick. Repeat the process each time, without hurrying. When you are succeeding with each kick, go through them again, but from further away and wider out.

HOW TO DO THE HAKA

The 'haka' is a traditional chanting dance of the Maori people of New Zealand. It is performed on ceremonial occasions, and is probably most famous because of the New Zealand rugby team, the All Blacks. They have been performing it at the start of rugby matches for more than a hundred years.

THE 'KA MATE'

The most well-known version of the haka is probably the Ka Mate (pronounced *'kah mah-teh'*), which goes like this:

> *Ka mate! Ka mate! Ka ora! Ka ora!*
> (It is death! It is death! It is life! It is life!)
> *Ka mate! Ka mate! Ka ora! Ka ora!*
> (I die! I die! I live! I live!)
> *Tenei te tangata puhuru huru*
> (This is the hairy man)
> *Nana nei i tiki mai, whakawhiti te ra*
> (Who fetched the Sun, and caused it to shine again)
> *A upane! Ka upane!*
> (One upward step! Another upward step!)
> *A upane, ka upane, whiti te ra! Hi!*
> (An upward step, another step, the Sun shines! He!)

GIVE IT YOUR ALL

The haka is best done in a group for maximum impact, so get the rest of your rugby team together to practise. A good haka is a loud celebration, with lots of chanting, thigh-slapping and grunting. You'll need to use your eyes and your tongue to make wild expressions, too, so don't hold back. This is a guide to a simple version of the haka for you to try.

Unbeatable tip. The haka is an important reflection of the respect and pride the Maori people have for their culture and heritage. It is taken very seriously, so make sure that anyone who gets the giggles gets their game face on immediately!

1. Stand in a group facing the same direction – towards the opposing team, for example. Your team will need to follow your lead at first, so make your moves big and confident.

2. With your legs wide, squat and puff out your chest, then stomp your heels rhythmically. Make your hands into fists, and bend your arms. Hold them out in front of your chest, with the right arm above the left. Hold them tensely so that they actually shake a little bit.

3. Make your eyes pop as wide as possible and roll them around in your head. Hang your tongue out of your mouth and flare your nostrils fiercely at the same time.

4. Now start chanting as loudly as you can. On pages 24 and 25, the words of the Ka Mate have been written out as you should pronounce them. Put extra emphasis on the words in italics. The corresponding actions are described in brackets. Follow them with lots of enthusiasm and energy.

5. (A) '*Kaah-mah-teh! Kaah-mah-teh!*' (Slap your thighs loudly on each '*kaah*'.)

(B) (Now look out fiercely at your opponents, arms out, ready to slap your chest …)

(C) '*Kow* rah!' (… slap your chest loudly on '*kow*'.)

(D) '*Kow* rah!' (Lift your hands up in the air, and look up to the sky on '*kow*'.)

6. Repeat step **5**, **A** to **D**.

7. (A) '*Teh* ney teh …' (Hold your hands in fists at your waist and punch forwards with your right hand on '*teh*'.)

(B) '… *tah*n gata.' (Punch forwards with your left hand on '*tah*n'.)

(C) '*Poou*-hou-rou …' (Now slide your right hand through the air, from your right hip to your left thigh on '*poou*'.)

(D) '… *hoou*-rou. *Naaah* nah neh-*eee* tee-kee-my. *Phah*-kah-phee-tee teh rah.' (Repeat slide on '*hoou*', '*naaah*', '*eee*', '*my*', '*phah*', '*phee*', and '*rah*'.)

24

8. (A) '*Aaah* ou-*paah*-neh!' (Slap your left forearm loudly on '*aaah*' and '*paah*'.)

(B) '*Kaaah* ou-*paah*-neh!' (Slap your right forearm on '*kaaah*' and '*paah*'.)

(C) 'Aah *ou*-pah-neh.' (Slap your left forearm once on '*ou*'.)

(D) 'Kah *ou*-pah-neh.' (Slap your right forearm once on '*ou*'.)

9. (A) 'Phee-tee …' (Scoop your right hand around in an arc under your left elbow.)

(B) (Like this.)

(C) '… teh-rah!' (Look up to the right and reach up with your right hand at the same time. Place your left hand on your hip.)

(D) '*He!*' (Slap your thighs one last time, then jump up in the air with a loud, grunting, '*He!*')

HOW TO SCORE THE MOST SPECTACULAR TRY

In a game of rugby, a 'try' is scored by outrunning all the other players, and carrying the ball over the goal line. You must 'ground' the ball (touch it to the ground) on the other side of the line for the try to be counted.

ADDED SHOWMANSHIP

You could just bend down and gently place the ball on the other side of the line to score your try. However, when you've broken through the last despairing tackle, accelerated past the last defender and the goal line is there for the taking, why not finish off your try in style? This will make everyone remember just how brilliantly you got there, and it will be the icing on the cake – an extravagant finish to cap a brilliant effort. Here's what to do:

1. It should all start at about three or four metres from the line, when you are certain you're going to score. Slow down slightly and get ready to dive.

2. Your dive needs to be as high as possible, so make sure there's plenty of spring in your legs.

3. Tuck the ball VERY firmly into your chest with one arm – you don't want to do all that work just to drop the ball or, worse, have it dislodged by your dive as you land. Your team-mates won't thank you for that.

4. As you hurl yourself up into the air, stretch one arm out in front of you, like a superhero. You can emphasize your

brilliance even more by extending your index finger in a 'Number One' salute. Adding a loud 'Whoop' as you go over the line won't hurt.

5. As you hit the ground make sure that the ball stays tightly tucked into your chest, and that the ball touches the ground to be certain that your try counts.

6. After you have skidded to a halt, and the referee has blown the whistle to confirm the try, throw the ball into the air as high as you can, as your team-mates rush to congratulate you.

HOW TO RIDE IN A RODEO

Rodeo competitions are based on the skills that generations of cowboys have used. Events include calf and steer roping, but the most spectacular and best-known are the riding events.

COWBOY SKILLS

Holding on with just one hand, you must ride a bull or a bronco (a horse that is not accustomed to a rider) for eight seconds to be awarded a mark out of a hundred. Here's how:

1. The bull will be penned in by the edge of the rodeo ring to keep it still while you climb on. As soon as you are astride the bull, wrap your hand firmly around the bullrope, which is wrapped around the bull's middle. It's a good idea to rub your hand with 'rosin' – a sticky substance that will give you a better grip on the bullrope, before you get on.

2. When the gate opens, the bull will rush out into the ring, bucking and jumping, trying to dislodge its unwanted guest (you). You must keep your balance, using just your legs and your hand around the bullrope, until eight seconds are up. Your other hand must not touch the bull.

3. Two judges will award points to you for how stylishly you ride, and to the bull for how well he bucks. 100 points is the maximum, but this is rarely, if ever, achieved, so don't expect top marks on your first outing – just give it your all.

4. For a better chance of staying on, lean back into the bull's jumps and bucks and use your free arm to help you balance. Get ready to make a run for it as soon as you fall off. Let the other cowboys bring the bull under control.

Unbeatable tip. In the USA you can learn rodeo skills from the age of eight and ride in special rodeos called 'Little Britches', with calves, young horses – even sheep! Steer clear of any local sheep though – they are unlikely to appreciate giving you a lift.

Warning. Be sure never to give this skill a try if you happen to be passing a bull in a field. Bulls are unpredictable creatures and best given a wide berth outside of a rodeo ring!

HOW TO BECOME A JUGGLING GENIUS

Juggling three balls is easier than it looks. In a few practice sessions you'll be well on the way to genuine juggling. If you can, use beanbags, or special squared-off juggling balls, which are easier to catch than ordinary balls. Perfect each step before moving on to the next – a good juggler is a patient juggler!

NO CLOWNING AROUND

To start with, practise with one ball only. This might sound too simple, but once you get the throwing pattern just right, the rest will follow much more easily.

1. Keep your hands level with your chest, elbows tucked in. Throw the ball up with a scooping motion, so that it follows a looping course from your right hand to your left hand (or left to right, if you prefer). The ball should follow an arc about 20 centimetres from your chest, just above your eye line.

2. Keep working with one ball for a while, making every throw exactly the same – same height, same trajectory, same speed – until you can do it without thinking. Switch hands, so that you can do exactly the same the other way.

3. Now it's time to add an extra ball. Start with one in each hand. Throw the first ball up, just as you've practised. When

the first ball is at the top of its arc, launch the other ball, as shown here. You should have just enough time to catch the first ball while the second is in the air. This is called the 'exchange'. It's the basis of the three-ball juggle. It's a good idea to get into a rhythm with this, because you'll need it when you move on to three balls.

4. Once you've perfected the two-ball exchange, it's time to move on to juggling more balls than you have hands. Hold two balls, lined up in your right hand (or left, if you prefer), one behind the other, and the third in the other hand.

5. As in the two-ball exchange, throw the front of the two balls in your right (or left) hand up. As it reaches the top of its arc, do the exchange, throwing the single ball up from your other hand, then catching the first ball.

6. Now launch the back ball from your first hand, and catch the single ball. This is a 'pass'.

Unbeatable tip. At first, doing one pass will be an achievement. Challenge yourself to do two in a row, then three and so on, until you can keep going for ages. Now it's time to challenge your friends!

HOW TO CYCLE
YOUR WAY TO VICTORY

When you enter a 'Grand Tour' cycling race, such as the Tour de France, one of the most challenging sections will be the mountain stages. They are also always the most exciting.

THE ATTITUDE FOR ALTITUDE

A great rider can make winning a mountain stage look easy. To be in with a chance you'll need excellent lung capacity. If you're lucky you might have naturally large lungs, but good training will help (try the Time-Trial Practice opposite). You'll also need a good 'power-to-weight' ratio – a combination of being light, but with very strong legs. Most of all, you'll need to be able to cope with the discomfort, even pain, of cycling hard up the side of a mountain. Here are some great ways to show your rivals how good you are:

• Break away from the other riders early on in the race and ride solo all day long. This is the most stylish way to do it as the cameras will be on you all the way, but it's by far the hardest, too. You need to strike a balance between getting away from the others as fast as possible, and getting so tired that they catch up, or all your hard work will come to nothing. This usually only works if the top riders in the main bunch don't really mind you winning the stage.

• Break from the main bunch with two or three other riders, and work together to stay away from your pursuers. This way you can save some energy to out-sprint your rivals in the final metres of the stage.

• Bide your time and stay with the leading bunch until a key moment, late in the stage – usually on a horribly steep part of the final climb – then go for glory with a solo break. Other riders will also want to try this one, so your breakaway has to be powerful and sustained.

TIME-TRIAL PRACTICE

Racing your friends on bikes is great fun, and perfect training to increase your lung capacity. Mark out a simple rectangular circuit on a grassy football pitch or in a park, so you can have fun and be safe if you fall.

You will need:

• two markers, such as cones, or sports bags
• a stopwatch, or a watch with a second hand • safety gear (helmet and knee and elbow pads) • paper and pencil

33

A 'there-and-back' time trial, or **'TT'** couldn't be simpler. Mark a start point and a turning marker by placing cones or bags on the ground about 50 metres apart. Record racers' times with a stopwatch. Each racer takes a turn riding around the turning point and back. The fastest time wins.

Unbeatable tip. The faster you go into a 180 degree turn, the slower and wider you come out of it. Take the turn at a moderate pace in order to get a tight line, without going wide of the turning marker, and be able to sprint out of the turn.

CRITERIUM CHALLENGE

A 'criterium' is a thrilling multi-lap bike race around a simple square or rectangular course. It's easy to mark out a course on a park or playing field, but if you have access to a public football pitch, for example, you have a ready-made course just waiting to be raced on – just follow the touchlines.

It's more fun and more exciting to have a smaller course and more laps, than a large course and fewer laps, so it might be better to use the pitch's halfway line as one side of the course, rather than racing around the whole pitch.

Decide on the number of laps you will do beforehand, set off together, and the first person to cross the finish line is the winner. When you have got used to the four-turn criterium, make things more interesting by building a little extension onto your course. Do this by adding markers to make a small extra square or rectangle on the longest side of your course.

Unbeatable tip. Don't try to break away from the bunch until the very end. Stay close behind your rivals, sitting in their slipstream and let them do all the work – then nip out just before the line and take victory in a cunning sprint finish.

34

HOW TO BE A STAR AT HANDBALL

Handball is an exciting, fast-moving, seven-a-side indoor game. The ball is big enough to bounce like a basketball, and just small enough to be thrown one-handed. The game has some similarities to football – the ball is thrown into a netted goal to score and passed between players – but you can also run with the ball by bouncing it, like in basketball. Players should not confuse this game with American handball, in which a small rubber ball is hit with the palm of the hand against a wall.

JUMP TO IT

A good jump shot will make you a star goal-scorer for your team. Here's how to achieve spectacular goals:

1. Take a run-up of three to four paces, then raise the ball to shoulder height.

2. Jump up and forwards, bringing your throwing arm back.

3. As your jump takes you wide of the defender, let the ball go as hard as you can. Aim for the floor just in front of the goalie, as this is one of the hardest shots to save in handball.

HOW TO TAKE A PENALTY

In a football penalty situation, the heat is on you, the penalty-taker, to score. If the goalie saves, he'll be a hero, and if you miss … disaster.

When you step up to take a penalty, there is bound to be some pressure on you and less on the goalie – after all, you'll look much worse if you miss the goal altogether. In a match situation you'll find you feel much calmer if you have practised your penalties over and over in advance, until you can score like clockwork. Sometimes even very skilful players miss penalties because of lack of practice or lack of focus, but when you have a clear idea of what you are going to do, and how to do it, successful penalties will come easily.

PENALTY OPTIONS

Research has shown that the most difficult areas for a goalie to defend are the top corners of the goal. However, if for instance the goalie happens to be very tall, he might be able to reach the corners easily. So you've got to have a plan B – a low shot into one of the bottom corners may be better.

Alternatively, if the goalie looks as though he is likely to dive early to one side or another, a fast shot down the middle would be a good plan.

As you can see, there are lots of options when it comes to taking a penalty. They can all work, so it's important that you practise targeting different areas of the goal. This way you'll be able to cover any eventuality confidently when you face the same situation in a match.

THE BACK OF THE NET

Practise penalties at your local park if nets are available, or in the garden. Alternatively, if you can find a large enough wall that you have permission to use chalk on, you could draw the outline of a goal to practise against. Try to aim for each corner in turn, using the inside of your football boot for better accuracy. You don't even need someone to act as goalie, although it saves time having someone kick your ball back to you.

Unbeatable tip. You must be decisive. Choose where you are going to place the ball, and stick with your decision! If you aren't 100% sure what you are going to do as you run up, there is a greater chance that you will miss.

HOW TO MANAGE YOUR FOOTBALL TEAM

It may just be a casual kick around in the park, but you still want to be on the winning side of a football match – and win in style, too. The team with the best organization will usually end up winning, even if the other side has one or two really skilful players. If your team can defend well and attack too, then you have an excellent chance of winning.

SHAPE UP

Generally, top football teams divide the ten players on the field into four defenders, four midfielders and two attackers (with the goalie making eleven). This is known as '4-4-2 formation':

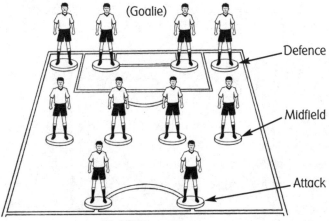

4-4-2 Formation

They also sometimes use a '4-3-3 formation', with three midfielders and three attackers, which is an out-and-out attacking formation, shown opposite:

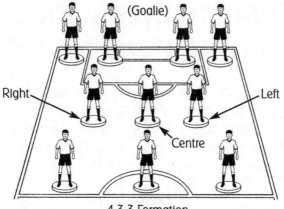

4-3-3 Formation

Even if you don't have a full eleven-player team to hand, you'll need to choose a shape, or formation, to play in, so that all areas of attack and defence are covered for ultimate success.

First, take a quick look around your side and agree between yourselves who will play in defence, midfield and attack – remember to take into account a player's particular skills. For instance, if someone is really good at scoring goals, they should probably play in an attack position.

Then divide the field into right, left and centre areas, facing your opposing goal. Split these areas between your defence, midfield and attacking players. At this stage it is very important that everyone agrees to their position and stays there, because each player has an important job to do.

Once positions and formation have been assigned, stick to them and practise, practise, practise – that way each player will know where their team-mates are, all the time. It will be much easier for team-mates to make successful passes and keep possession of the ball.

HOW TO KEEP A BALL IN THE AIR FOR HOURS

Bouncing a standard football on your knees, feet and head without it touching the ground, or 'keepie-uppies', is an impressive skill that you can easily achieve with a bit of practice. You may not want to go for a record-breaking 24 hours, but it will certainly improve your ball-handling skills.

GOOD KNEE CONTROL

A good way to improve ball control on each foot is by doing a 'kick-bounce' drill. Here's how:

1. Kick the ball in the air, let it bounce once on the ground, then kick it up in the air again, and repeat. Remember to switch legs regularly, so that they both improve – gradually your feet and legs will become stronger.

2. When you get good at using both feet, try to kick the ball up to head height, and tap the ball up with the area just above your forehead to keep the ball going. You can even use your shoulders, too.

3. Whenever you feel ready, just leave out the bounces, using your knees, feet shoulders and head to keep the ball off the ground for as long as you can.

40

HOW TO COMMENTATE ON A MATCH

A good commentator adds passion and excitement to a sporting event. You don't necessarily need to be good at the sport you commentate on, but you do need to love it and know as much about it as possible.

Different skills are required for television and radio commentating. For example, if you are commentating on a football match on the radio, you need to paint a good visual picture for your listeners who cannot see what is going on. You might say:

> 'Smith has passed the ball across to the right of the pitch, where Jones traps it and tries to find a space ....'

While on TV your role is to add to what the viewers are already seeing, so you might say:

> 'That was a pinpoint cross-field pass by Smith. Now Jones has the ball, what can he do with it?'

SEND ON THE SUBSTITUTES

The key to a more exciting commentary is a great vocabulary. Start a list of words that you'll need for your chosen sport, then think of as many alternatives for each of them as you can. This way, instead of saying a cricketer has 'hit' the ball, you could, in various circumstances, use words like 'nudged', 'deflected', 'whacked', or 'swung at'. As you come across new words and expressions, add them to your list and commit them to memory.

41

Practise your technique by watching your chosen sport on television with the sound turned down. Add your own commentary to the event – make it as thrilling and entertaining as you can. You might want to do this by yourself at first, but as you gain confidence, try it out on friends and family, so that they can tell you where you need to improve.

PLAN AHEAD

Preparation is everything. Use this list to check you are fully prepared before each match or game:

• Learn the names of all the players or competitors and make sure you can recognize their numbers.

• Make sure that you know how their names should be pronounced.

• Memorize any relevant facts and statistics about previous matches that you could use to add extra detail.

• Build up your sporting vocabulary to keep things interesting.

• Listen carefully to how other people commentate.

• Let your voice show excitement and emotion with different tones to add interest.

• Don't be afraid to raise your voice and even shout if the occasion demands it.

HOW TO BE A TIDDLYWINKS HOTSHOT

Tiddlywinks is a highly competitive game of skill and strategy … and a bit of luck, too. Each player has a 'squidger' which is a large plastic disc, and six smaller plastic discs, called 'winks' – four small and two medium-sized. Winks come in red, blue, green or yellow – for a two-player game you will have two sets of winks each. The object of the game is to get all of your winks into a central pot by using your squidger to press down on the edge of a wink. This makes the wink pop up into the air, hopefully towards the pot. The player who gets all of their winks into the pot first, wins.

POTTING TECHNIQUE

Hold the squidger at an angle of about 45 degrees and press down on the middle of the wink. Still pressing down, draw the squidger back towards you. As it flicks off the edge of the wink, the wink will pop up and forwards into the air.

The angle you hold the squidger at will affect the distance that the wink jumps. If you want it to go higher and land closer to you – if your wink is very close to the pot for example – you should hold the squidger at an almost vertical angle. The further away from the pot you are, the more horizontal the squidger will need to be – you should also add extra pressure to give your wink a boost.

Experiment with this technique so that you can judge the angle correctly in the excitement of a tiddlywinks tournament.

SQUOP IT

If you are lucky, or skilful, enough, one of your winks will land on top of one of your opponent's winks. This is a 'squop' and it means that your opponent is not allowed to play their wink until it is uncovered again. To achieve a squop you'll need a gentle precision shot from close range. Players use various techniques, but this is an effective method to practise:

1. When your wink is close to your opponent's, position yourself so that you are closest to his wink, with your wink on the other side. Angle your wink away from you, so that the edge touching the table is furthest from you.

2. Gently stroke your wink from the centre to the furthest edge, making it hop in towards you very slightly, covering your opponent's wink.

HOW TO BE THE GREATEST GURNER

The World Gurning Championship takes place each autumn, in Egremont, England. For hundreds of years, contestants have been judged on their ability to make the most grotesque and distorted faces possible. As a competing 'gurner' remember that you'll be judged on the difference to your usual face, as well as the weirdness of the end result. Being normal-looking to start with actually gives you an edge.

THE GURN FACTOR

• Before competing, try out your best gurns at home in the mirror. Ask friends and family to rate them so that you can choose the worst possible expression for the championship.

• Many gurners have false teeth, which they can remove, allowing them to fold their features into even uglier extremes. If you're waiting for any adult teeth to grow, use this to your advantage for an extra gurn-factor.

• Past winners have given their facial creations names such as 'Quasimodo' and 'Popeye' – give your own gurn a great name to sum it up for the judges.

• When it's your turn, pop your head through the traditional horse's collar and give the crowd a good gurn!

HOW TO CONQUER YOUR FRIENDS AT CONKERS

Conkers is a game for two players, played in the autumn when conkers start to fall from horse-chestnut trees. You and your opponent each have a conker, pierced and hung on a string. You then take turns to hit each other's conker, the aim being to destroy your opponent's conker. You need accurate hitting skills, and, vitally, the hardest conker.

A WINNING CONKER

Choose several fairly large, evenly shaped conkers and put them in a bowl, or a sink, full of water. The ones that float to the top are less dense, therefore less tough, and so potential losers. Throw them away.

Some people swear by soaking a conker in vinegar. You could even gently bake your conkers in the oven to harden them (although many people regard both these ideas as cheating). If you are extremely patient, you could even keep them in a dark place for a year to harden up.

GET IN THE GAME

1. To prepare your conker for battle, make a hole through the middle with a skewer (get an adult to do this bit for you) and run a shoelace or a piece of string, about half-a-metre long, through it. Tie a big knot at the end to hold the conker on safely.

2. To claim the right to strike first, quickly shout, 'Obbly, obbly onker, my first conker!' before your opponent has the chance to do the same.

3. Wrap the end of the string around the fingers of your strong hand. Hold the conker itself in your other hand and stretch the string out tight, bracing the string with your thumb. Your opponent should hold his conker out, dangling from its string, ready for you to hit.

4. Take aim at your opponent's conker, and release your own conker from your fingers as you flick your arm down quickly. Thwack! If the two strings get tangled, the first to shout 'Strings!' gets the next shot.

5. You then take turns to hit each other's conker until one starts to crack and disintegrate.

47

HOW TO TRAIN LIKE A CHAMPION

Some sports-people are so dedicated that they'll train all day, every day, even on Christmas Day. However, don't be fooled into thinking 'more is better'. The most successful athletes always follow three crucial rules in their training:

1. Only do the right training for your fitness level. Don't overdo things if you are training to improve your fitness, but don't slack off if you're fit enough to find training easy. So, not too much, not too little, not too hard, and not too easy.

2. Have a plan of progress that allows your training to increase as you get fitter.

3. Allow recovery time – when you are resting and sleeping your body has a chance to make the changes that improve fitness. Without rest, you can't get stronger or train harder.

Every part of your life can be part of your training. From the food you eat before and after training, to how you organize your schedule, and making time to relax. You should try to reduce anything that stops your progress to championship status, including bad food and late nights.

You may not be able to control everything that affects your training, but even an uncomfortable bed that stops you getting a proper night's sleep is worth changing. If you can eat right, make sure your training is at the right level, and get plenty of sleep, you'll soon be on your way to being a champion.

HOW TO SPIN A BASKETBALL ON YOUR FINGER

This is one of the coolest tricks to try to do with a basketball. It looks great, and it's much easier than you think.

SPINNING SKILLS

The trick is to get the ball to spin fast enough that it stays on the tip of your finger – even if it's only for a second or two. Here's how:

1. Hold the ball firmly, with your hands either side of it. Spin it by flicking your hands quickly in opposite directions. Make sure you're not throwing the ball up into the air.

2. Don't worry about getting the ball on your finger yet, just get it moving nice and fast and let it fall to the ground the first few times.

3. Now it's time to get to the nitty-gritty. As before, hold the ball up and give it a good spin. This time quickly get your index finger underneath the ball, making sure it's rigid, and roughly in the centre of the ball.

You might drop the ball a few times, but as you practise, you'll find it easier to spin the ball faster and find the centre until it sits on your fingertip for several seconds at a time.

HOW TO TAKE A FREE THROW

Silence falls on the basketball court – all eyes are on you as the referee hands you the ball. Bounce it two or three times to build up a rhythm and get comfortable in front of the crowd. Concentrate – look up at the basket, aim ... and whoosh, the ball drops through the hoop.

Or at least it should. Taking a successful free throw in basketball is all about practice, so that when you face the same situation in a game, you are able to do so easily, just as you have hundreds of times before.

AND THE CROWD GOES WILD

A good free throw comes not just from your hands, but also from an upward motion that starts from your knees and finishes with a good follow-through from the wrist and fingers. Here's what to do:

1. Stand with your feet shoulder-width apart. Your stronger foot should be slightly forwards, aiming at the hoop. Bend your legs a little, and bounce the ball a few times to get a feel for it.

2. Lift the ball in front of your face, holding it in your strong hand, elbow tucked in, and keeping it steady with your other hand. Keep your knees bent.

3. With your wrist bent back and ready to fire, take aim. Target the back rim of the hoop, so that you have a good chance of the ball falling through.

4. To shoot, come out of your bent-knee position so that your whole body moves upwards a little. Use this energy to propel the ball towards the hoop with a flick of the wrist. Don't take your eyes off your target.

5. Make sure you follow through with a flick of your wrist and fingers, then just wait for the whoosh.

Unbeatable tip. A good way to get going on this is to start fairly close to the basket. Try some shots, get used to the rhythm and feel of your free throw, and develop some accuracy. Then gradually work backwards until you are shooting from the free-throw line.

HOW TO WIN A THUMB WAR

Absolutely anyone can win a thumb war. The goal is simple –
just pin down your rival's thumb for four seconds. Here's how:

RULES OF THUMB

Agree the rules before you start, to ensure a cheat-free match
and no arguments. For instance, arm twisting is not allowed,
and you must not use any other fingers in the war.

1. First, stand facing your opponent, then hook your fingers
together, leaving your thumbs free. You will be at a
disadvantage if your opponent is right-handed and you are
left-handed, so suggest alternating which hand you use.

2. Now both of you should chant, '1-2-3-4, I declare a
thumb war!' while tapping out the countdown with your
thumbs by switching them from side-to-side.

3. You must attempt to trap your opponent's thumb under
yours, but only by moving your own thumb around. It will
help if your thumb is longer than his, or if you are more
flexible. Let battle commence!

Unbeatable tip. Tempt your opponent by keeping your
thumb still, and letting him think he can pin it. As he stretches
his thumb out, it's there for you to pin, but be super-quick!

HOW TO TAKE A HURDLE

Sprinting over hurdles is great fun, but very demanding. You'll need to be flexible, well co-ordinated, and have good balance. Build up to it gradually with the simple steps described below.

There are standard hurdle heights for different ages, and if you're lucky enough to have access to an athletics track, you will be able to use these for practising your technique. You could also use mini-hurdles, known as 'banana steps'. Otherwise, you can make your own practice hurdles.

You will need:

• a child's garden chair
Or, • 2 large plastic plant pots • a one-metre-long
bamboo cane • modelling clay

Make the most of any good weather and head out to the garden or a park for some practice. For practice purposes your hurdle does not need to be very high – anywhere between knee and mid-thigh height is okay. If you are using a chair, make sure the seat of the chair is facing towards you. Otherwise, place your plant pots upside down on the grass, roughly a metre apart. Divide your modelling clay into two lumps and place them on top of the pots, then secure the ends of the cane in the clay to form your practice hurdle.

HURDLING ACTION

In hurdling, you have a 'lead leg' – the leg that goes straight over the hurdle in front of you – and a 'trail leg' – the leg that you swing round behind you. Here's how to get used to the hurdling action with your trail leg first of all:

1. If, for example. you are leading with your left leg, your right leg will be your trail leg. Stand with your right leg just behind the left side of the hurdle, with your left leg to the side. Slowly swing your right leg over the hurdle, so that it goes from behind the hurdle to in front of it. Repeat this several times. This will develop your flexibility and balance, and give you a feel for the height of the hurdle.

2. When this feels comfortable, progress to walking up to the hurdle, and swinging your trail leg over it as before. When you have got the hang of this, try jogging slowly up and repeating the motion.

NOW THE LEAD LEG

Here's how to get used to the hurdling action with your lead leg. Again, let's assume your lead leg will be your left leg:

1. Walk forwards, and every 4 to 5 steps lift your left knee as high as you can in front of you. You can use mini-hurdles for this too, stepping over each hurdle with as high a knee as possible.

2. When you have practised this a few times, repeat, but lift your leg straight ahead of you as high as you can – again, over mini-hurdles if possible.

3. Then practise the straight-leg lift at jogging pace, lifting your leg out in front of you every 4 to 5 steps. You'll probably notice that the arm opposite the lead leg – in this case the right arm – naturally comes up.

WHAT DO YOU GET?

Now you have an idea of how your lead leg and your trail leg will work, it's time to put them both together and hurdle. Using a mini-hurdle, or a small chair, approach your hurdle at a jog and … hurdle it. Your goal is to 'run over' the hurdle rather than 'jump over' it – this means taking the hurdle in your stride instead of slowing or 'stuttering' before going over it. When you are comfortable getting over a single hurdle, you can set up two hurdles a few metres apart and practise at a jogging pace. Try to work out how many strides you need between hurdles, so that when you set up a third hurdle you know where to set it.

HOW TO CROSS THE FINISH LINE

You've made your final lung-bursting effort over the last few metres of a marathon. Your legs are burning, but victory is yours. You just have to cross the line in style. Here's how.

DOS

• 'Dip' – leaning forwards at the last moment. If you think it's a close finish, a well-timed dip will get you over the line first.

• Wave to friends and family, if there's time.

• Raise your arms in the air and smile.

• Run right through the tape, so that it snaps and pings up spectacularly.

• Wait until you have broken the tape before you collapse, if your effort has been that great.

DON'TS

• Try not to dip so low that you fall flat on your face just before the line.

• Never start to celebrate too early and slow down – letting someone pass you with a metre to go.

• If you're meant to do a lap of the stadium before finishing the race, make sure you do so – there's nothing worse than thinking you've won when there are still 400 metres to go.

HOW TO 'WORK THROUGH THE PAIN'

Exercise and sport can be very strenuous – they're supposed to be – and, in general, the harder you work, the better you'll do. So how do you know how hard to push in a cross-country race, or a track race, such as the 800 metres, for instance?

First of all, it's important to tell the difference between the feeling of working hard and the feeling of an injury about to happen. Breathlessness, a tight chest, slightly achy legs and general discomfort are all due to fatigue.

They are your body's way of trying to suggest it would like a nice lie-down on the sofa. If you are to race well, you have to learn to deal with them. The first thing to remember when you start to feel fatigued is that it is natural – and everyone else is feeling it, too. That boy who is racing a couple of metres ahead of you and looking comfortable – he's suffering, too.

PAIN SCALE

If you are racing cross-country, for example, one strategy you could use is to rate your discomfort on a scale of one to ten, where ten would be so much you would collapse on the ground. The more you race and train, the better you will be able to rate your discomfort. If you are running along and feeling like it is hard work, rate it. You might find that your discomfort really only scores six out of ten – so in fact you could push a bit harder. If it rates nine out of ten, you are probably at your limit, and it might be best to ease back a little. Be honest!

A second strategy is to make yourself keep going at that level of discomfort as far as a visible landmark that is 100 to 200 metres away – such as a tree – then when you get there, reassess how you are feeling. If you are able to carry on, then set yourself another point to run to. This way you might be able to keep running hard right to the finish line, just by breaking your race down into small sections.

Finally, if you're feeling fatigued during a race, then it's because you are working hard, so instead of saying, 'This is bad,' say, 'This is just how it has to feel for me to do well.' And remember how great you will feel when it's all over and you've won, hopefully.

WHEN TO STOP

A sharp pain, in your knee or ankle for instance, means you are about to get an injury and it must not be ignored. Stop running and tell your coach or parent.

HOW TO BECOME A CHEESE-ROLLING CHAMPION

The annual cheese-rolling race is held every spring at Cooper's Hill in Gloucestershire, in England. A large Double Gloucester cheese (weighing up to four kilograms) is released at the top of the hill. As a chaser you are aiming to catch the cheese, but as it travels at over 100 kilometres per hour, there's almost no chance of actually doing this. Instead, the first down the hill and over the finish line wins the cheese and all the glory.

This may sound simple, but Cooper's Hill is so steep that it is impossible to run all the way down. In places, cheese-chasers simply let themselves fall, roll, or slide.

You will need enormous amounts of courage, the willingness to take a risk and a great love of cheese! The quickest way to win is to just hurl yourself down without regard for life or limb, and hope that you arrive at the bottom in one piece.

HOW TO BE A SUPERSTAR BOG SNORKELLER

The World Bog-Snorkelling Championship is held each summer in the Welsh town of Llantwrd Wells. The race takes place in one of two 55-metre-long ditches, and consists of swimming to the end and back in the fastest time possible.

You will need:

• a face mask and snorkel • flippers – the bigger the better

THE 'RULES'

No swim stroke may be used – just kicking in a straight line through dark, muddy, murky, weed-infested water.

A wetsuit will help, because it helps you to float, allowing you to go faster, but in the true spirit of bog snorkelling, fancy dress is encouraged.

Don't set off too fast. It's surprisingly hard work, and you need to keep some energy for the return length.

POOR-VISIBILITY PRACTICE

What's tough about bog snorkelling is the lack of visibility – you probably won't be able to see your hand in front of your face. So practise swimming short distances at your local pool with your eyes closed. You may not be allowed to use a snorkel, so come up for air regularly. Make sure there is no one in your way and you are not next to the pool wall, or there may be an unpleasant crash.

1. Start in the shallow end, and take a deep breath.

2. From a standing position, dive as far forwards as you can, arms extended in front of you in a streamlined position, one hand on top of the other.

3. Kick hard in a straight line and make sure your breathing is relaxed.

4. Keep your legs fairly straight as you kick – if you bend too much at the knees you reduce your forwards motion.

5. When you complete a length, turn as quickly as possible and set off again.

Go eight kicks with your eyes closed, lift your head to see where you are, and adjust your line if necessary, then carry on – eight more kicks with your eyes closed, and so on.

HOW TO COME FIRST IN THE CORNFLOUR CHALLENGE

This is a great way to bamboozle a friend and win a bet. Challenge a friend that he can't get a pound coin out of a bowl of liquid in five seconds. It's not as easy as it sounds.

STICKY FINGERS

The trick is that the liquid is a mixture of cornflour and water. This combination has the strange property of getting more solid the harder you push into it. Here's what you need to do:

1. First put 500 grams of cornflour into a large mixing bowl and slowly add water, stirring until you have a thick, custard-like consistency.

2. Bring your friend into the kitchen, and show him the bowl of liquid. Ask him to give you a pound coin, and provide one of your own. Drop both coins into the bowl. Get your watch, or a stopwatch, ready to time him.

3. Now challenge him to get one of the coins out in five seconds. If he succeeds, he can have both coins. If he doesn't, you keep both. He will probably try to grab a coin as quickly as possible. The faster he moves his hand, the harder the liquid will set around his fingers, making it impossible to get a coin out.

4. To win the bet, dip your hand very slowly into the mixture, and gently fish out a coin. You'll have to practise this a few times on your own to get the hang of it and make sure you can do it in less than five seconds.

HOW TO THROW A BALL

Being able to throw a ball accurately is a vital skill in many sports, from baseball to cricket.

TARGET PRACTICE

Follow this handy guide to hone your throwing skills:

1. To throw well overarm, you must have a stable base. This means that as you prepare to throw, your legs should be apart, not close together, and your knees slightly bent. With a stable base to throw from, you stand a better chance of a strong, well-directed throw.

2. Aim your non-throwing side at your target – your left side, if you are right-handed, your right side if you are left-handed.

3. Point your non-throwing arm at your target as you pull the hand that is holding the ball back behind you. This helps you 'sight' the target and gives you balance, too.

4. As you throw, bring your arm up quite close to your head. so that it is almost vertical. If your arm comes out too wide you'll have less chance of throwing straight.

5. Hold the ball loosely in your fingers, not tightly in the palm of your hand. This allows your wrist and fingers to guide the ball on its correct path, and allows the ball to be released easily from your hand.

Unbeatable tip. It will help to have your wrist 'cocked' – slightly bent back – as you take your arm back, and to flick your wrist through as you release the ball. This helps the ball follow the path you want it to. To begin with, this motion may make you throw the ball downwards a bit, but with practice you will get the timing of the release right.

HOW TO HIT THE CRICKET STUMPS

The opposition's star batsman hits the ball and sets off for a run – but you swoop like a falcon, pick up the ball and throw it straight at the stumps! He is run out, his team collapses without him at the crease – and you are the hero.

WINNING WICKETS

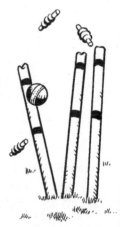

When you're trying to hit the stumps and run a batsman out – particularly if you're close to the wicket and running in the direction of the stumps – an underarm throw is your best bet. It's easier to be accurate, and you can release the ball more quickly. Here's how:

1. Approach the ball on the ground in quick, short strides, bending your knees and your back as you get to the ball. You might need to slow down a little – nothing looks sillier than completely overrunning the ball.

2. Pick up the ball with your throwing hand near, or on the outside of the same foot (the right foot if you throw right-handed, for instance). Keep your head over the ball and your eyes on the ball.

3. As you come upright, swing back your throwing hand. Keep your head down, but now look at the stumps.

4. Release the ball quickly towards the stumps, with the palm of the hand following through on a direct path for as long as possible.

5. Shout *'Howzat!'* as the rest of your team congratulate you happily.

HOW TO SPEED UP YOUR CATCHING SKILLS

Excellent reflexes are very useful, especially if you are born with them. If you're not the best at catching already, just try these practice drills. You'll soon be able to catch the ball every single time.

Practise with a tennis ball, and, when you feel more confident, switch to a smaller, bouncy rubber ball for an extra challenge.

DRILL ONE

1. Stand 1.5 metres from an outside wall. Throw the ball at the wall fairly hard, so that it rebounds straight back at you.

2. Catch the ball with both hands until you get the hang of it. Then throw the ball so that it comes back first to your strong hand, and then to your weaker hand.

3. Increase the difficulty by either standing slightly closer to the wall, or throwing the ball a little harder. This way you will have slightly less reaction time, but your goal is still to catch the ball. At first it may seem impossible, but after a while your reflexes will speed up and you will succeed.

DRILL TWO

1. Stand 2 to 3 metres from the wall. Shut your eyes and throw the ball in a gentle loop so you have a good idea of how it will come back.

2. See how long you can leave it before you open your eyes and successfully catch the ball. As you get better at it, throw the ball a little harder, so that it comes back faster.

HOW TO GIVE A WINNING WINNER'S INTERVIEW

Your life's dream has just come true, and, after years of dedicated training, you've crossed the line at the New York Marathon in first place. Cameras surround you, there are microphones in your face, and journalists jostle each other to get close. Now is the time to be a role model for your sport.

DO

• Smile as much as possible – look happy.

• Congratulate your competitors – say how good they were and how hard they made you work.

• Say thank you to your coach, your parents, your training partners, everyone who supported and helped you get here. You'll probably have a company that sponsors you for your shoes and kit, so you'd better thank them, too.

• Even when the interviewers ask a really obvious question (such as, 'How do you feel?'), answer with enthusiasm.

DON'T

• Say it was easy-peasy lemon squeezy.

• Pretend not to be out of breath.

• Say how awful your competitors were.

• Reply to the interviewer by saying, 'What a silly question!'

HOW TO WIN
THE CAPTAINCY

Some team captains are loud and energetic, others are calm and focused, but all good captains have the respect of their team, as well as being good at their sport. You'll need to …

… show that you care about the game – turn up early to training, be prepared to help the coaches get kit ready, and help supervise younger players.

… become one of the best players (although not necessarily the absolute best).

… have a good knowledge of the game's rules and tactics.

… motivate the players around you using positive language, not negative language (for example, say, 'Keep going, you're doing well,' rather than, 'That was rubbish!').

… be diplomatic – be able to give criticism, but always in a nice way. Being bossy or rude doesn't make you a good captain.

… show that you are determined to win, but know how to be fair.

… always set a good example – train hard, play hard.

… always make it clear that you want to lead the team in order to help everyone win, rather than for your own glory.

HOW TO MAKE THE MOST OF THE WELCOME HOME

Whether you've won a brace of gold medals, or triumphed at the FA Cup Final, there's nothing quite like a home-town welcome to complete your moment of glory.

• You'll probably be on the upper deck of an open-top bus, so cram as many people up there as you possibly can.

• Keep a hand on the trophy so that all the photos have you in them.

• Wave flags and scarves from the bus so that the fans know you've won the trophy for them – never miss an opportunity to applaud them and thank them.

• Enjoy every second – it may never happen again.

HOW TO FINISH ON A DOUBLE IN DARTS

Darts is a sport in which sharply pointed missiles are thrown at a target – the dartboard (shown opposite). This means you should never play without adult supervision in case of injury, although alternatively, magnetic versions are available.

SETTING UP

Your board must be safely fixed to the wall, so get an adult's help. The centre of the board (the 'bull's-eye') is traditionally 5 feet, 8 inches from the floor (or 1.73 metres), with the number 20 at the top. The line you throw from is the 'oche' (pronounced *'ocky'*) and it should be 7 feet, 9 and a quarter inches (or 2.37 metres) from the board. You could mark this on the floor with masking tape, which is easy to remove later.

RIGHT ON TARGET

Start by practising your throwing technique. Here's what to do:

1. Hold the dart with the grip between your thumb and forefingers (either one, two or three of them). Bend your elbow and tilt the dart back slightly, so that it will curve in an arc when you throw it.

2. Keep your eyes on the board, bring your arm back and quickly forwards. Release the dart as your arm moves forwards. Follow through with your hand towards the target. (Don't flick your wrist as this may move the dart off course.)

Once you get the hang of hitting the board, start trying to aim for specific sections of the main circle.

THE BOARD

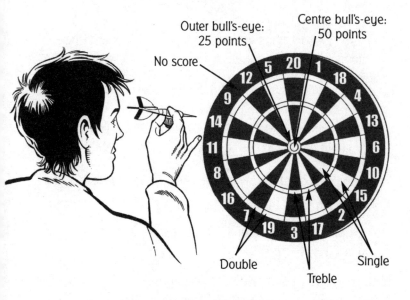

Centre bull's-eye: 50 points

Outer bull's-eye: 25 points

No score

Double

Treble

Single

RULES OF PLAY

• The only way to win a game of darts is to finish on a double (or a bull's-eye), so it's very important that you can hit these. As you get more comfortable with your technique, start focusing on the outer ring, where the points you score are double the number of that segment.

• For most players, the easiest doubles to finish on are usually 16 (scores 32), 8 (scores 16) and 20 (scores 40). You'll soon discover that you can hit some numbers more easily than others, too. Make sure you remember which ones are your best doubles for when you play a match.

• Competitions are usually played one-on-one, starting with 501 points. For a friendly match at home, it's more usual to start with 301 points. The aim is to reduce your score, taking it exactly to zero with your last turn.

• Each person plays with three darts, giving them three throws per round. First, take turns to throw one dart, aiming for the bull's-eye – the person who gets their dart the closest, starts.

• Take turns to throw all three of your darts, trying to score as highly as possible to reduce your points quickly.

• You must *never* throw a dart when anyone else is in front of the oche.

• If your dart falls out of the board before a count of five is up, it doesn't score.

• When your score is getting close to zero you need to start calculating your finish. If you can, you should work out a way to use one of your best doubles to give yourself an even better chance of winning. For example, if you need 52 to finish, and your best one is a double 16, you would want to throw a single 20 first, then a double 16 (because 20 plus 32 is 52). There are many, many different combinations that can be used to finish a game of darts, so in order to become an unbeatable darts player, you'll need to make good calculation a top priority.

Unbeatable tip. One of the great things about darts is that strength, height and weight aren't very important. This means that you can take on and beat older players if your throwing is accurate, and you're good at calculating your finishes.

HOW TO BE A HIT IN HOCKEY

Hockey is an exciting team game with eleven players on each side. Goals are scored by whacking a small ball into your competitors' net with a curve-ended hockey stick. Mastering the skills described here will make you a better player, and instantly put you at the top of the coach's selection list.

DRIBBLING SKILLS

You can dribble the ball in two ways – closely, to make yourself hard to tackle, or quickly, to make yourself hard to catch. You need to keep your stick away from your feet and out in front of you, so that you can pass the ball quickly when you need to. Here's how:

1. Hold the stick with your hands apart. Your strong hand should grip the stick firmly, lower down the stick, but your top hand should be more relaxed.

2. Keep your knees bent and your back leaning forwards, so that your head is nearly over your stick-head.

3. Move forwards, keeping the ball in contact with your stick as much as possible, so that you are almost rolling the ball along with the stick-head.

4. To go faster, tap the ball out in front of you, rather than rolling it smoothly along the ground. Your stance should be a little more upright, and your head will need to be higher, so that you can move faster.

PUSH PASS

A 'short corner' in hockey is like a free kick on the edge of the box in football. There's a really good chance of scoring a goal, but it all has to start with perfect delivery of the ball to the 'stopper', who stops the ball for the next player to take a shot at goal. That's where you come in with the 'push pass'.

The ball has to travel quickly, accurately and smoothly to the stopper. Here's what to do:

1. Hold the stick with your strong hand fairly low down, about 30 centimetres from your top hand.

2. To make a wide and stable base for your push, stand with your feet well apart and your knees bent. You should have a little more weight on your back foot.

3. Point your front foot at your target (the stopper's stick) and place your stick behind the ball.

4. Keep the head of your stick in contact with the ball as you move your weight from your back foot to your front foot. Push the ball towards your target. Start slowly, then increase the speed of the stick-head's movement.

5. A long follow-through will ensure an accurate and quick push – just what your team needs.

HOW TO POT THE BALL

For a perfect pool shot you need to know how to stand, hold the cue and line up your shot just right. Combine all three at once and you'll be clearing the table in no time. Here's how:

RIGHT ON CUE

1. Hold the cue gently in your strong hand. Make a 'bridge' with your other hand on the felt surface of the pool table, with your fingers spread and your thumb held in close to make a groove for the cue to follow.

2. Stand slightly side-on to the cue so you can pull it back smoothly. The cue should draw an imaginary line through the centre of the cue ball (the white one), your target ball, and the pocket. Bend down to look along it. Experiment with different angles to hit the target ball just right.

3. Once you are lined up, keep your eye on the target, and pull the cue back slightly. Your elbow should be at a right angle, with your arm in line with the target. Push the cue forwards, tap the cue ball, and remember to follow through.

HOW TO MASTER ORIENTEERING

The aim of an orienteering race is to use a compass, a map and your wits to get around a set course. You must decide the best way to tackle the route, reaching a marked set of control points in the correct order, as quickly as you can.

Courses at organized events are colour-coded according to the level of difficulty, so you can decide how hard the challenge will be for you. There are also events – coded white – just for children and families.

PARK PRACTICAL

Setting up your own course is a great way to hone your orienteering skills. Take turns with your friends to plot a route around your local park and race each other for the fastest time.

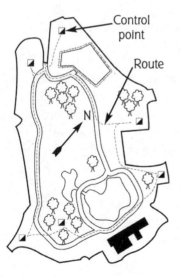

Control point

Route

N

1. To take your bearings with an orienteering compass (shown opposite), hold the compass level until the needle settles. One end of the needle, usually red, will point north. Rotate the dial until the north orienting arrow lines up with the north end of the needle.

2. Turn your map until the north line on the map lines up with your compass bearing. You should now be able to match landmarks on the map to what you see around you.

3. If you want to go in a particular direction – the next control point, for instance – line the compass up so that the direction-of-travel arrow points towards it.

4. Now rotate the dial until the orienting arrow lines up with north on your map.

Orienteering Compass

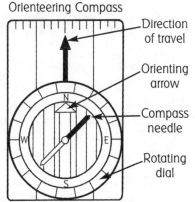

Direction of travel

Orienting arrow

Compass needle

Rotating dial

5. With the direction-of-travel arrow pointing in front of you, turn yourself until the needle lines up with the orienting arrow. Walk forwards and you'll be heading in the correct direction, although you should reorient yourself regularly – each time you reach a landmark, for instance.

MAPPING METHODS

Your skills play as big a part as your fitness in orienteering – it's even nicknamed 'cunning running'. Use these tips to become the most cunning runner in your family.

• Hold your map so that what is in front of you on the course is in front of you on the map. For instance, if you are walking towards some trees 100 metres away, hold the map with the trees near the top.

• Use your thumb to mark your position on the map. Whenever you reach a landmark, such as a footpath or a stile, reposition your thumb to remind you where you are.

• Each time you get to a control point, check the number to make sure that you are finding them in the correct order – it would be terrible to have to go back on yourself!

HOW TO BE A GREAT HIKER

Walking is one of the simplest and best forms of exercise there is, and a great way for you and your family to explore nature. However, first and foremost you need to be safe, so make sure you follow these pointers for the best outdoor experience.

GET KITTED OUT

• Clothes in heavy cotton fabrics, such as denim, are fine for home, but don't work well for hiking. They absorb water very easily – if you get drenched on a hike wearing jeans you'll get very wet, very quickly, and you'll stay wet. The same rule applies when it gets very hot, and you perspire. Choose clothing in specially made 'breathable' fabrics instead, as they allow your sweat to escape more easily.

• Follow a layering principle and take several thinner items of clothing, rather than one thick jumper, for instance. This way you can add or take away layers as you cool down and heat up. Several thin layers also protect you from the cold better than one thick top.

• Your hiking boots should be comfortably worn-in before attempting a hike. Wear two pairs of socks to avoid blisters.

• Your rucksack should also be as comfortable as possible. Better to have one that fits you than the latest, smartest-looking one that feels awful after an hour.

OUT AND ABOUT

• Before you set out, check that a family member has packed a mobile phone and a basic first-aid kit, as well as water and snacks, such as dried fruit and nuts, or 'trail mix'.

• On country lanes without pavements walk on the right, so that you are facing the vehicles coming towards you. An exception to this is when you are approaching a tight right-hand bend (the road is curving to the right in front of you) when it makes sense to cross to the other side so that you get a better view of traffic coming around the bend.

• Walking in the hills is especially good for you if you walk briskly enough to be aware of your breathing and your heart pumping. However, if you are embarking on a long walk, especially a very hilly one, always set off at an easy effort – not walking too quickly. If you run out of energy when you are a long way from your end point, at best you will have an unpleasant end to your walk, and at worst you may get stranded by the weather or by night falling.

HOW TO DROP IN ON A SKATEBOARD RAMP

If you've been skateboarding for a while now, you might have already mastered a few tricks, such as an 'ollie' or a 'frontside 180', and be able to ride down shallow slopes without falling too much. You may want to take things to the next level, so off you go to the skate park and look longingly at the ramps, with everyone rolling confidently up and down.

TAKING THE PLUNGE

Put on your helmet, and knee and elbow pads, before you get going. You want to drop in with everyone else, but you don't know how and you don't want to feel foolish, so follow these tips to learn how to attempt the 'half-pipe' for the first time with confidence:

1. Don't be over-ambitious. It makes sense not to start with the steepest, biggest ramp in your area – find one that is less steep on which to practise your technique.

2. Take your skateboard to the top of the ramp and put the tail of your board on the coping (the metal rail that runs along the edge of the ramp). Hold it down firmly with your back foot, so that your board is sticking up and out over the ramp.

3. With your weight on your back foot, place your front foot gently on the board directly over the front wheels.

Keep your knees slightly bent.

4. Before you can over-think the situation and start worrying, push your front foot down, without lifting up your back foot.

5. Keep yourself centred over the board as you drop down the curve of the ramp. Try not to lean back too much and make sure your knees are still bent – you're in!

Unbeatable tip. Even with a great sense of balance, it will almost certainly take you a few goes to get the hang of dropping in. You will probably fall at least a couple of times before you master it – just keep working at it!

HOW TO THROW AN AMERICAN FOOTBALL

The quarterback in American Football is one of the most important players on the team. One of his jobs is to pass the ball to the right player at the right time, so an accurate throw is vital. The best quarterbacks make this look easy – a lazy flick of the arm and the ball speeds through the air with pinpoint accuracy.

ON THE GRIDIRON

With a bit of practice you'll soon amaze your friends with your own throwing skills out on the 'gridiron' (the field). Here's how:

1. First, grip the football in your throwing hand. Use your fingertips rather than the palm of your hand. Your fingers should sit between each loop of the lace that runs down the middle of the ball. This will help to give you a firmer grip.

2. Don't worry if your hands aren't big enough to grip the ball in the middle – hold it towards the point and use your other hand to help maintain your grip on the ball.

3. Stand side-on to your target, with your front foot pointing at it, and your throwing arm to the back. Bring the ball up near the shoulder of your throwing arm, and pull your arm back, keeping your elbow bent and your hand close to your head. If you are aiming to throw the ball a very long way, lean back slightly and lower the shoulder of your throwing arm. For a shorter throw, keep your shoulders even.

4. If you can, hold the ball with just your throwing hand. This way you can line up your pass by stretching your other arm out in front of you, pointing at your target. Otherwise, it's better to keep a good grip on the ball and just keep your eyes on the target.

5. Throw the ball by whipping your arm forwards, following through with your shoulder, wrist and hand in one smooth movement. As your weight transfers from your back foot to your front foot, step into the throw with your whole body to give it extra power.

6. Let the ball go with a snap of your fingers. This will help the ball 'spiral', so that it cuts smoothly through the air, rather than wobbling madly. Follow the curve of the throw through with your wrist and hand to improve your aim.

Unbeatable tip. Remember, if you are throwing a pass for a running receiver – a moving target – aim for the position you think he will be in as the ball comes down.

HOW TO BE A SUPER-STRONG SWIMMER

Sometimes even when you can swim really well, your stroke can lack a little bit of 'oomph', and other swimmers still get ahead of you. So where can you get the extra power that will have you swimming away from your rivals? From your legs.

VERTICAL-KICK DRILL

This special drill is guaranteed to make your kicking stronger, your legs more powerful and your stroke faster – especially for front crawl and backstroke. Rather than holding onto a kick-board and propelling yourself along the surface of the water you'll be holding yourself vertically in the water with the power of your legs alone. Supporting your own bodyweight just by kicking requires more power and is more difficult, but it really is worth the extra effort. Here's what to do.

1. First, head for the deep end, or to a point where you are just out of your depth, so you don't hit the bottom of the pool with your toes. Make sure a lifeguard is present and ask an adult to supervise you when you're in deep water.

2. Now tread water. This means keeping yourself upright in the water in one place, instead of swimming along. Use your arms to support yourself and a breaststroke kick – like a frog – to keep your position.

3. When you feel ready, begin vertical kicking by switching to a front-crawl kick – scissoring your legs back and forth. Keep your kick 'narrow' so that your legs don't go a long way in front or behind your body.

4. Use your hands at your sides to 'scull' the water gently – cupping them to scoop the water in small, circular movements. As you get stronger, cross your arms over your chest – then try with your hands held up at shoulder height. The toughest challenge is to keep kicking with your arms stretched up over your head.

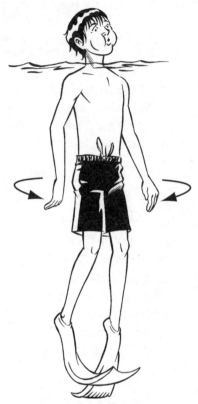

5. Kick fast and hard, so that your chin stays above the surface. If you feel yourself moving downwards, start sculling again. Remember to keep your legs fairly straight – don't lift your knees or let them bend too much. Keep your toes pointed down.

6. Kick hard for five seconds, then grab onto the side of the pool or the lane rope and rest for 10 to 15 seconds, then kick again for five seconds. Repeat five times. As you get better at it, try to extend the time you kick by five seconds.

Unbeatable tip. When you start using this drill, it may seem difficult to keep your head above water. Wear fins on your feet to get you started (if you are allowed at your local pool), or hold on to the lane rope with one hand until you are stronger and more confident.

HOW TO PERFECT A RACING DIVE

At the start of a swimming race, split seconds are crucial. A good racing dive will get you off the starting block further and faster than everyone else, and guarantee you a place on the swimming team.

ON YOUR MARKS

When you practise, set yourself an imaginary target where your hands will enter the water. Once you have achieved it several times, push yourself to dive that little bit further away from the edge of the pool. You'll soon be way ahead of your rivals.

1. Stand with one foot forwards and one foot back, as if you were going to set off running. Then bend and grip the edge of the starting block.

2. Now bend your knees, so that you are crouching slightly. Lean back, or rock back very slightly, so that you are ready to put the maximum effort into your push-off.

3. When the race begins, hurl yourself forwards and upwards. Height is important so that you go as far forwards as possible. The higher and further you can travel before hitting the water, the better – you travel much faster through air than through water.

4. Place one hand on top of the other and stretch your arms out as far as possible. Your legs should be straight and your toes pointed. This is a 'streamlined' position, which reduces wind resistance as you fly through the air.

5. When you enter the water, your body should be as long and streamlined as possible so that you travel further under water before you begin your stroke. In mid-air, some swimmers point their arms downwards, some straight ahead. Experiment to see which works best for you.

Unbeatable tip. Once you enter the water you'll need to keep up the good work with a super-strong swimming stroke. Check out the drill on page 84 to make sure you get the race sewn up.

HOW TO WIN AT ELEPHANT POLO

Traditional polo, on horses, has been played for hundreds of years. It is a fast and furious game in which riders gallop madly around a field astride polo ponies. Players must swing long polo mallets at a ball, trying to score goals. The elephant version of polo has only been around since the early 1980s, and is played mainly in Nepal, Thailand and India. It's far from fast and furious though – while polo ponies are swift, agile and can turn easily, elephants are slower, and less nimble.

YOU ARE NOT ALONE

When you play elephant polo, you will have a '*mahout*', who is like a jockey, who guides the elephant for you on the field of play. It is your job to concentrate on hitting the ball with your mallet. The mahouts generally only speak Nepali, so it'll help in your quest for success to learn some basic Nepali commands. These may prove useful:

'*Sahayao garnus*' – 'Help!' Or, '*Roknuhos*' – 'Stop!'

TOP TACTICS

• Get a long mallet. You're a long way off the ground when you're sitting on top of an elephant, so you'll need an extra-long polo mallet to reach the ball with.

• Bigger means slower. All the players have to choose their elephant before the game starts. If you want to speed about the field, pick the smallest elephant on offer – it will be the fastest.

POLO POINTERS

• Don't worry about falling off your elephant – if you do, the game will be stopped while you remount.

• Don't be tempted to let your elephant lie down in front of your own goal – that's against the rules!

• Don't let your elephant pick up the ball with its trunk – you'll concede a penalty.

Unbeatable tip. You can give your elephant sugar cane or rice balls packed with vitamins after the game, and your mahout a cold drink, but not the other way around.

HOW TO BOWL A STRIKE

A 'strike' in ten-pin bowling means knocking over all ten pins with one shot. Repeat this spectacular feat over and over and your score will go up and up – the points you get in the frame following each strike are doubled. Use these top tips to achieve super-striker status among your friends.

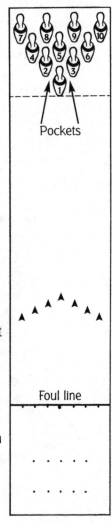

CHOOSE THE RIGHT BALL

Choose the heaviest ball you can lift with the thumb and second and third fingers of one hand. More weight gives more power to your shot. Make sure the holes are big enough – you don't want to get a finger stuck and go flying after your ball!

'X' MARKS THE SPOT

To find the right starting point, take four paces away from the 'foul line', then turn to face the pins. If you are right-handed, line up your left foot with the large dot marking the centre of the lane (line up your right foot if you are left-handed).

For a pin-point perfect strike, right-handers should target the 'pocket', or gap, between pin one and pin three. Left-handers should aim for the pocket between pin one and pin two. Line your shot up with the shoulder of your throwing arm, as the ball will come from that side of your body, not the centre.

TAKE A SHOT

1. On the first step (with your right foot if you are right-handed, your left foot if you are left-handed) lift the ball up in front of you, lining it up with your target. Use the arrows marked part way down the lane to help guide you.

2. Swing the ball back on your second step – be careful not to accidentally let go at this point. As you take your third and fourth steps keep your eyes on your target and use the ball's momentum and your own forwards movement to swing your arm forwards.

3. Release the ball just as you are about to bring your hand back up. The weight of the ball pulling on your hand will help you know when to let go. A long, strong follow-through is vital to keep the ball on line, so bring your hand up in line with your target.

X
'Strike!'

Watch those pins crash to the ground!

Unbeatable tip. Take care not to let your foot go over the foul line, as your strike will not count. The lanes are also kept nice and smooth with regular oiling, so chances are you might take a tumble, as well.

91

HOW TO SWING LIKE A WINNER

The game of golf is hundreds of years old and still one of the most popular sports in the world. Whether you want to play with friends on a local course, or become a prize-winning player, you'll need to start with getting a good swing.

'FORE!'

Hitting a tiny ball with a golf club may seem impossible (it's not), but hitting it accurately is key. The swing itself is very complex, so follow these tips to be on your way to golf gold.

1. Stand side-on to the ball, with your feet shoulder-width apart, so that you'll swing straight along the line you'd like the ball to follow.

2. Hold the club with your stronger hand below your weaker hand, with your strong hand overlapping the thumb on your weaker hand. The club should be angled from the bases of your little fingers towards the tips of your index fingers. Make sure that your grip is light, so that you don't transfer any tension from your hands to your swing. Keep your head still, and the face of the club head aiming squarely at your target.

3. Start your swing by smoothly rotating your hands, arms, shoulders and hips away from your target. As your club goes further back, rotate your shoulders, as well.

4. Swing your club around in a smooth arc, keeping your head still and your eyes on the ball at all times.

5. Don't stop when you hit the ball – keep swinging – a good follow-through is vital to keeping the ball on target.

PUTT-PERFECT PRACTICE

All you need to practise putting is a putter (a club for close-range shots), a golf ball and an old mug. Practise on carpet, for an even surface, similar to the smooth grass of a golf green.

1. Place the mug on its side, roughly two metres from your putting position, then place the ball on the carpet and stand to the side.

2. Line up your shot, with your weight balanced evenly on both feet. Bring the club back just a few centimetres, keeping your arms and shoulders moving as one.

3. Gently swing the club forwards to hit the ball. The club, and your arms and shoulders should all move at the same time and the same speed. As you hit the ball, keep your head still and don't move your wrists forwards.

Once you have the hang of it, remember to increase and decrease your putting distance. Keep practising until you can get the ball safely into the mug every time.

HOW TO STAND OUT IN THE TEAM PHOTOGRAPH

The problem with most team photographs is that you'll probably all be wearing a uniform, and may even be covered in mud, so it's much harder to get noticed. When you look back at the picture in years to come, you'll want to be able to spot yourself immediately. Here are a few top tips to guarantee you stand out from the crowd:

• Use some gel to spike your hair up as high as it will go.

• Put your shoulders back and lift your head up to make yourself look taller.

• Turn slightly, puff out your chest and look straight at the camera, like a model.

• If you're likely to be covered in mud when the photo is taken, have a spare uniform stashed, ready to change into. This way you'll look spotless and sharp compared to everyone else, and you'll definitely get noticed.

• At the moment the photographer takes the photo, open your eyes as wide as they will go and grin like a chimpanzee.

• As a last resort, hide a fluorescent-green clown wig under your shirt. Just as the photographer is about to take the shot, whip it out and put it on your head. Unbeatable.

HOW TO TEAR A PHONE BOOK IN TWO

It's an ultimate 'show of strength', but there's a trick to tearing a phone book in two. You can easily do it with a little practice.

STRONGMAN

1. Choose a thin phone book to practise on (an out-of-date one might be best). Grip the top of the phone book firmly, with your hands quite close together, near the centre.

2. Bend the book in the centre and squeeze the pages into a 'V' shape away from you. With your thumbs close together, grip the V tightly between your fingers and thumbs, squeezing the paper firmly. As you squeeze, the pages will separate slightly at the point of the V.

3. Press your thumbs down and apart to start a tear.

4. Keeping a very tight grip on the phone book, push down with one hand and pull up with the other to make all the pages start to tear. Keep ripping!

95

HOW TO GIVE A PRESS CONFERENCE

You might be talking about a great victory or a shattering defeat, your first international or the end of a glittering career, but in any press conference, the best thing you can give a gathering of expectant journalists is a quote to remember.

POINTS FOR THE PRESS

• If a journalist asks you a long, involved question, don't just answer 'yes' or 'no' at the end of it – you'll avoid having uncomplimentary things written about you if you consider your answer seriously.

• The glare of TV lighting and flashes from photographers' cameras will be distracting, but try not to frown, as it will make people think you are grumpy.

• Think about the kinds of questions journalists might ask, and prepare a few answers in advance that aren't boring clichés. Make them laugh, make them think, make them sit up and listen, and your press conference will be a memorable success.

HOW TO BUILD STRENGTH

No matter what sport you play, 'resistance training' – pushing or pulling against weights – will help improve your strength. It doesn't have to involve weights at a gym though – one of the best ways to get stronger is by using your own body weight. The exercises below are simple to do, don't have to take a lot of time, and need no equipment.

Each time you do one exercise – a press-up, for instance – that is one 'rep' (repetition). A group of reps, ten for example, is a set. Do several sets of each one, with a short rest between.

Press-ups. Place your hands on the floor, shoulder-width apart, and hold yourself up on the balls of your feet, with a straight back. Lower yourself down and up again. (Use your knees instead of your feet if you can't hold yourself up.)

Squats. Standing with your legs wide and your heels flat, bend slowly at the knees to a sitting position, then straighten your legs again. Don't bend forwards too much.

Forward lunge. With your feet parallel and your arms at your sides, step forwards with one foot and lower yourself until the knee of your other leg is nearly touching the floor. Raise yourself up again, keeping your back vertical at all times. Change legs for each set you do, and do an even number on each.

Burpees. Squat down on the floor like a frog, with your knees under your chest and your hands on the floor. Kick your legs straight out behind you – add a press-up here, if you like – jump your legs back in and jump up in the air.

Front plank. With your hands gripped together and your elbows shoulder-width apart, lean on your forearms, bracing yourself above the floor on the balls of your feet. Your neck, head and body should make a straight line. Hold the position for a count of ten.

SIMPLE CIRCUITS

To begin with, you'll need to rest between sets, but as you get stronger, rest for less time. A gold-star performance would be to do three sets of all five exercises without resting – a 'circuit'. Alternatively, try these variations. Rest between exercises if you need to, before going straight through the whole circuit.

• Simply try doing each exercise for a set time, say 30 or 60 seconds, before moving on to the next.

• For an added challenge, gradually increase the number of reps in each set. For instance, you could do three press-ups, and rest, followed by six press-ups, and rest, followed by nine press-ups, and rest, finishing with twelve press-ups.

To make your training effective, you'll need to work out the number of reps and sets for each exercise that challenges you. It shouldn't be too easy, or too hard. Add extra sets, or increase the number of reps you do as your strength increases. Doing a strength circuit three or four times a week is excellent, but even once a week is much better than nothing at all.

Unbeatable tip. It's a good idea to change the order you do the exercises in, ideally every three to six weeks. This is because your body gets used to doing things in a certain order, and stops adapting. Mixing things up a bit will refresh your muscles, and make sure your training is still effective.

HOW TO SPEED SKATE

If you can already ice skate and love to race, then speed skating is for you. What you need to get started, and do well, are skill, strength and staying power – a set of speed skates and the one-piece aerodynamic speed-suit could probably wait until you're more advanced. Pads and a helmet are an essential, though – even rookie speed-skaters move quite fast.

COOL LEANINGS

You'll need to practise the perfect skating posture to get yourself up to speed – leaning low to the ice, with one arm tucked behind you for a more aerodynamic shape.

One of a skater's key skills is taking corners at speed. To do this you'll need to learn the 'crossover'. Cross your outside leg in front of the other around the curve, and lean to the side. You might even brush the ice with your fingertips, if you're going fast enough!

Unbeatable tip. Take extra care of other skaters when practising your speed techniques. Check to see if there is a speed-skating club at your nearest rink, where everyone will have the same speedy interests.

HOW TO TAKE ON AN EXTREME SLED RACE

The bobsleigh race is incredibly fast. There's just a sheet of fibreglass between you and the solid ice as you hurtle around tight bends. And at speeds of over 150 kilometres per hour, you'll have just split seconds to steer a course.

If your dream is to be part of a four-man or two-man bobsleigh team in the Winter Olympics, then you'll need to prove that you have plenty of speed, power and guts. If you're already displaying these attributes, and you love the thought of whizzing down an icy course at speed, then the bobsleigh might just be for you. However, teams have been known to cross the finish line on their heads, so you'll have to keep yours!

LUGE LONER

If you're more of a lone wolf, but still love speed and danger, then get on to a luge. This is a thin fibreglass shell with two metal runners. You lie on your back and steer with your legs and by shifting your weight slightly. This requires a great deal of concentration, because one tiny slip

100

can mean a massive wipeout – and on a luge there are no brakes.

SNOW, GO!

If you're lucky enough to live in an area where you get regular winter snow, you'll be able to get a taste for these two winter sports by simply taking out your sledge, or sled, next time there's a good covering.

If your sledge has steering ropes, then simply pulling on one or the other will make it change direction. If your sledge is a bit more basic, you'll need to lean your body slightly left or right to make the sledge turn. You can also let one foot lightly graze the snow to increase resistance on one side, causing the sledge to move in that direction.

Using this method means you are in a good position to brake with your feet if your sledge is going too fast. (If all else fails, just lean right off the back of the sledge and into the snow for an emergency stop.)

SAFER SLEDGING

• Check that your sledge is in good working order before you set out.

• Wear a helmet and never sledge head-first.

• Check that the area where you plan to sledge is not icy, and that there are no tree stumps, rocks or fences to crash into.

HOW TO BECOME A MUSHING CHAMPION

There's nothing quite like the rush of cool air on your face as you race across a snowy landscape, pulled by a team of loyal huskies. Of course, to become a true sled-dog champion, you'll need guts, stamina and an excellent sense of balance – as well as some seriously warm clothing!

PUPPY POWER

A sled-dog race is usually run as a 'time-trial', with each team of dogs and their 'musher' (that's you) setting off separately.

As a serious musher you'll not only need to be a real 'dog person', but also have a range of other skills, including dog training, sled handling and outdoor survival techniques. Many races take place over several days, in sub-zero temperatures, so it's vital for you to be able to stay the course.

Your ultimate challenge will be the 'Iditarod' in Alaska – a race covering nearly 2,000 kilometres, which can take more than two weeks to complete. Even if you come in last you get a special prize – the Red Lantern – because just to complete the race is a huge achievement.

SLED-DOG SPEAK

You'll have a team of up to 16 huskies, hooked up in pairs to pull your sled, with your fastest, cleverest dogs in the lead. To have any hope of completing the course, you'll need a great relationship with your dogs and some basic terminology to point them in the right direction. Here's what to say:

Mush! / Hike! .... Start running

Haw! .... Turn left

Gee! .... Turn right

Come haw! / Come gee! .... Turn 180 degrees, left or right

Whoa! .... Stop (add a pull on the brake, too).

Unbeatable tip. For truly authentic-sounding sled dogs, you might like to name your team of dogs using one of the native Alaskan languages. Consider names such as *Magukuk* (howls at the moon) or *Nanuq* (polar bear) to get you started.

HOW TO SERVE AN ACE

Top tennis players can serve the ball at speeds of up to 240 kilometres per hour, sending it whizzing by an opponent, giving him no chance to return it. This is called an 'ace'. It's the most commanding way to win a point, and a great way of taking control of the game from the outset – so take your time, and make it count.

SENSATIONAL SERVING

Before you can serve an ace, it's best to know how to serve. Here's what to do:

1. First, stand sideways on to the net, with both feet behind the baseline (the furthest line from the net). Your back foot should be parallel with the net, but your front foot should be pointing towards it. Each time you serve the ball it must land in the service area (the rectangle on the other side of the net) diagonally opposite where you are standing.

2. Hold the ball in one hand and the racquet in your strong, serving hand, a bit like you're holding a hammer.

3. Take a couple of practice swings first, pulling the racquet back behind you and swishing it over your head in a smooth arc. This will give you an idea of how high to throw the ball so that your racquet connects with it.

4. Now practise throwing the ball up to that spot, so that you can be sure of getting it to the right height each time. Your throwing arm should be quite straight, and you should aim to throw the ball just a few centimetres in front of you.

5. Now the tricky part – you need to combine both movements so that you hit the ball with the centre of the racquet at just the right moment.

6. Make sure that you follow through on your serve with a slight snap of your wrist, so that the ball lands safely in the service area.

7. Remember to run forwards into the court as soon as you have served the ball so that you are ready to hit your opponent's return shot.

POWER PLAY

Once you've got the hang of a nice rhythmic service action, it's time to add power, speed and accuracy – the perfect combination to achieve an ace. Here's what to do:

1. Imagine you are about to throw a ball as hard and as far as you can. You'll need to take your arm back further, bend your knees a bit more and move your feet apart, as well as mentally preparing for the extra effort. It's just the same when you want to add power to your serve.

2. Practise a normal serve two or three times, then add in the elements above. Take your serving arm back further, bend your knees as you throw the ball up, and bring the racket round with more speed as you hit the ball.

3. When you feel as though your serve has a lot more force behind it, get to work on its accuracy. On an empty court, place markers, such as sheets of paper, where you want to serve the ball. Take a few minutes each time you play to practise getting better at hitting them.

ACE SERVICE STRATEGY

It's no good hitting a super-powerful serve and having it come straight back at you. Think about whether or not your opponent has a weak side, too. For example, if he is right-handed, with a weak backhand, and you are serving to his 'deuce court' – the one to your left – then a service down the centre line will get you your ace.

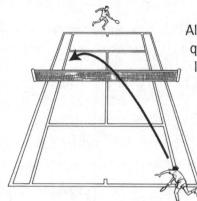

Alternatively, if your opponent has quite a strong backhand, or is left-handed, aim to serve towards the tramlines running down the edge of the court. This will target his weaker side, and give you a much better chance of serving an ace.

Unbeatable tip. When you are getting ready to serve, check where your opponent is standing. Look to see where there is more room to direct the ball, and target that area. Hopefully the ball will be harder for him to hit.

HOW TO BOUNCE BACK FROM AN INJURY

If you play a sport, it's quite likely that you will get an injury of some sort sooner or later. Here are the two kinds you may get:

• An 'extrinsic' injury – for example, a twisted ankle or a broken arm – comes from an external cause (such as a collision or a fall).

• An 'intrinsic' injury – a pulled hamstring or a sore Achilles tendon, for instance – comes from too much training or effort.

In both cases, the first thing you need is a healthy dose of patience. Don't try to start your sport again before it is safe to do so – you may well make your injury worse and have to stay away from your favourite sport even longer.

If you have an extrinsic injury, it's usually a case of waiting patiently until it gets better, and you'll know when it's better because it won't hurt any more. If it's a more serious injury, such as a broken arm, then of course your doctor will give you exactly the right advice to follow.

For most injuries, remember the acronym, '**RICE**' as soon as you realize that you have a problem.

DO ...

Rest – stop playing or training.

Ice – apply ice to where it hurts.

Compression – add pressure –
a compression bandage can help.

Elevation – elevate the part that
hurts into a comfortable position.

DON'T

• Stretch strained muscles.

• Massage strained muscles for
around 48 hours after the injury.

• Forget that time is the best healer.

• Pretend to all your mates that
you're fine and play a game when
it will make the injury worse.

HOW TO DEAL WITH YOUR ADORING FANS

Once you hit the big time as a sporting star, you're bound to get more attention from your fans – it's only natural. Successful sports-people will always be heroes to lots of people.

It will feel great, but you mustn't let the adoration go to your head. You may not have time, in any case – there'll be press conferences, media breakfasts, photo shoots, sponsorship obligations, fans clamouring for your autograph and trying to pat you on the back as you go to and from training – all very exhausting. You might wonder why you wanted to be a sports-star in the first place!

You'll have to remind yourself that you're in a privileged position, and the adulation is just part of the package.

The best way to deal with it is to make it a two-way thing – try to give back a little of what you get. Sign autographs, thank people for their support, encourage other young people to play your sport, and help charities. That way you'll feel so much better about all the glory and adoration you receive.

HOW TO SPIN SERVE AT TABLE TENNIS

To bamboozle your table-tennis opponent right from the outset, learn how to put spin on your serve. You can use top-spin, side-spin, back-spin – even side-back-spin – so they won't know which way the ball will bounce.

In table tennis, the serve must bounce once on your side of the net then once on your opponent's side. You can serve long or short, hard or soft, spinning or straight, and to add to the fun, you can serve backhand or forehand. It's up to you. You don't even have to serve to a certain area of the table, as you must do in tennis.

In table tennis, it's very rare to serve an ace – usually the best serves set up an easy second shot – which is why a tricky, spinning serve is very useful.

SPIN IT!

Here's how to achieve a good forehand serve, with added backspin. This will be the hardest serve for your opponent to return.

1. Stand at 45 degrees to the table, with the ball in the palm of your hand.

2. You should hold the ball behind the end of the table, and 15 centimetres above it.

3. Toss the ball straight up – it must travel at least 16 centimetres into the air – and take your bat backwards and upwards.

4. Move the bat forwards and down as you strike the ball, but holding it at an angle of 45 degrees beneath the ball – this will make it spin backwards.

5. Aim for the ball to bounce closer to you than to the net.

Unbeatable tip. Practise with different speeds and amounts of spin – but remember, the closer the ball lands to the net on your opponent's side, the harder it will be for him to get it back to you.

HOW TO BE A TEAM PLAYER

Being a member of a team means that you have to care more about what's best for everyone than you do about yourself. The saying, 'There's no "I" in team,' sums this up perfectly – if you play as part of a team, you only win if your team wins.

YOU SHOULD ...

- Know your role within the team.

- Know what your team-mates' roles are.

- Support your team-mates if they make a mistake – it's a normal part of playing any sport.

- Assist and encourage your team-mates.

- Do your best for the team, not for yourself.

For example, late in a football match, with the score level, you get the ball in front of goal, in a fairly good position. However, your fellow attacker moves into an even better position and waves for the ball.

You could ignore your team-mate and try to go for the goal yourself – after all, you had the ball first – or, you could give up the ball and let him try. If you miss, your team will feel let down, but if you pass the ball to him, and he scores, you will have helped your team to win.

There is a great difference between each member of a team playing as well as they can individually, and each team member making sure they play as well as they can for the whole team's success.

HOW TO TAKE ON THE BEST, AND BE BETTER

The best way to be better than your opponents is to … well, just be better, but in the long term trying to win is not as good as trying to do your sport as well as you possibly can at that exact moment in time. Here's how to achieve this.

If you focus just on winning, you are thinking about the future (even if it is only a few minutes in the future, it is still the future). This will mean that you aren't concentrating 100% on what is going on RIGHT NOW. If you aren't concentrating on your game, then it's likely you will not be doing it as well as you could. That means you are less likely to win.

If you put all your effort and concentration into playing as well as you can, at every single moment of the game, you stand more chance of winning. So if you think about winning, you are less likely to win, and if you don't think about winning, you are more likely to win. Try it – it works!

113

HOW TO PERFECT A BATON CHANGE

A relay race is run over either 100 metres or 400 metres, with four runners on each team. You must race to be the fastest to pass the baton safely around the track. A slick, seamless baton change can make the difference between winning and losing a medal, so it's vital to practise to get it right on the day.

BATON, AND ON, AND ON

The baton is a metal tube measuring about 20 centimetres long. If you don't have a real baton handy, practise with the tube from a roll of kitchen towel instead. Here are the key points to work on:

The handover. Each section of the relay is called a 'leg'. The person running the first leg holds the baton in his right hand – the person on the second leg holds out his left hand to take it. The second-leg runner passes the baton from his left hand into the third-leg runner's right hand. Repeat the pass from right hand to left hand in the third and fourth leg. This way, each person always knows where the baton will be. It won't matter how fast everyone on your team runs if you can't get that baton safely around the track.

The exchange zone. This is a 20-metre section marked with two coloured lines on the track. The baton can only be handed over here, or your team will be disqualified. Make sure everyone is familiar with where it starts and finishes, and how long it takes to run out of it. Timing is key!

HANDING OVER

1. As you approach the exchange zone call to your team-mate to start running. Don't slow down.

2. Press the baton down firmly into your team-mate's hand. Don't hold it for him to grasp – he can't see it.

RECEIVING

1. When you hear your signal to go, set off at full speed. Trust your team-mate and your practice sessions.

2. Reach behind you, with your palm held up flat, ready for the baton – don't look back.

3. When you feel the baton pressed firmly into your hand, grip it tightly and fly.

Unbeatable tip. When waiting to receive the baton, don't run too soon or your team-mate won't be able to get the baton into your hand. There's nothing worse than watching the baton clatter to the track, especially if your team was in the lead!

115

HOW TO HOP, STEP AND JUMP TO VICTORY

Triple jump is one of the most popular field events in athletics, because it is both complex and spectacular.

LEAPS AHEAD

To be a great triple jumper you'll need to be fast, strong, well-balanced and good at jumping, obviously. Here's what to do:

1. Start with a short run-up of about ten strides when you are practising – you can extend it as you get better at the combination of hop, step and jump. Halfway through your run-up, increase your speed, so that the last four paces are the fastest. This will prepare you for the take-off (the hop).

2. Take off from your strong foot, trying to reach out with your leg as you land (on the same foot) ready for the step.

3. Take the biggest step you can with your other leg, taking it as high as you can for maximum distance. Imagine it as more of a leap, than a step, if that helps!

4. Once you land the step, gather your arms and extend them to assist your effort to move forwards and upwards, as you jump forwards with both feet.

5. Try not to fall backwards as you land, as this will reduce the final length of your jump.

Through each of the three phases, keep your head up and your eyes focused on your final landing point. Don't look down at your feet.

TRIPLE-JUMP DRILLS

As well as practising the actual triple-jump sequence, doing these drills will help improve your strength and balance, and make the triple jump itself easier.

Two hops, one step. Simply repeat two hops and one step, driving each knee up high every time. Keep going for about 30 metres, rest and repeat.

Barrier hop. To develop better leg-strength, use a low hurdle to practise hopping over. As an alternative you could even try hopping up onto the first or second step of your staircase at home, which will work just as well.

HOW TO GET THROUGH YOUR MEDALS CEREMONY

Everyone deals with this big occasion differently. Chances are you'll be overwhelmed by emotion and excitement at being on the winner's podium, so just remember these top tips to point you in the right direction during your big moment.

• Try to accept the flowers they give you with good grace – everyone else has to – then plant a huge kiss on your medal and hold it up for your fans to see.

• If you can, sing along with your National Anthem as your flag is raised to the top of the stadium.

• You could hold one hand over your heart to show an extra sense of passion and pride in your sport and country, or stand with your hands clasped behind your back.

• It's completely acceptable, after all your hard work, to break down into sobs of joy, relief and fatigue. It shows how much the medal means to you (and you won't have to remember the words to the anthem).

• Remember to turn any tears into a huge smile as the crowd cheers you at the end – wave or punch the air as you turn slowly in a full circle, for everyone's photos.

HOW TO LOOK LIKE A CHAMPION

You know how some sports-people just look like winners all the time – cool, confident and unfazed by the pressure? Sometimes these people can make their opponents feel a bit nervous just by their appearance.

One of the things about great champions is that they are not only talented at their sport, they train with great dedication, too. If you know you are well prepared for a game or a race, then you feel confident and relaxed, alert and aware. And if you feel confident, you look confident. If you feel relaxed, you look relaxed – just like a champion does.

A good way of expressing this confidence is to tell yourself that you CAN do what is needed to win, or to help your team win. Picture yourself doing these things successfully, and at the same time say positive things to yourself, such as:

'I can pass the ball accurately.'

'I can keep up a strong pace right through the race.'

'I can score when I get the ball in front of goal.'

When you start to think positively and clearly about your own performance, and you get more confident about it, you'll stop worrying about your opponents.

That's when you start to look like a champion.

HOW TO BECOME A WORLD-RECORD HOLDER

John Naber is a former swimmer from the USA. At one Olympic Games he watched a team-mate win several gold medals and break a world record. He realized that to do the same thing himself he would need serious training and careful planning. As soon as he got home, he and his coach sat down and worked out how fast he would need to swim at the next Olympics to win, and break a world record himself. It was about five seconds faster than his best time.

The swimmer and his coach then divided that increase in time by the number of weeks to go before the next Games – he had about 200 weeks. Splitting the five seconds by 200 they realised that if he could swim 0.025 of a second faster each week over the next four years he would win gold and break the world record. And that's exactly what he did.

SETTING TARGETS

This is a perfect example of how you can break down a goal into achievable amounts – bit by bit you move forwards, getting faster, stronger, or more accurate, until you arrive at your target. It could even be your own world record.

Think about what you want to achieve, whether it's improving your sprint-start times, increasing your goal-scoring accuracy, or getting a more powerful tennis serve. Decide how to go about doing this, taking advice from your coaches or parents, and set yourself a reasonable time limit. Be determined, stick with your plan, and you'll get there, just like John Naber.

HOW TO BE THE 'ULTIMATE'

Ultimate Frisbee is a highly competitive sport with similar rules to netball (you can't run with the Frisbee disc once you've caught it) and American football (points are scored by catching a pass in your opponents' 'end zone'). It's a non-contact sport, and unique in that matches have no referees. Instead, players follow a code of conduct, and self-referee the game.

THE ULTIMATE FIELD

The diagram below shows the measurements of a standard field of play for Ultimate. With seven players to a team and a large playing area, it involves a lot of running, jumping and diving for the disc, as well as accurate throwing and good strategy.

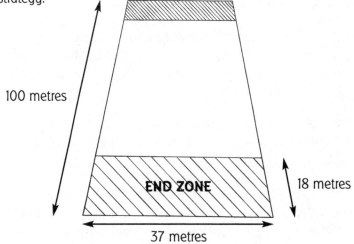

100 metres

END ZONE

18 metres

37 metres

You can easily adapt most sports pitches to the game – just use the scoring areas at either end of a football pitch or basketball court, for example, as your end zones.

THE ULTIMATE GAME

First decide which team will start the game in defence (trying to stop the other team scoring) and which team will be offence (in possession of the disc, trying to score), by using a coin toss, or perhaps a quick thumb war (see page 52).

1. Each team lines up in front of their own end zone and a member of the defence team throws the disc to the offence team to start. Players should each 'mark' a member of the opposing team to try to stop them passing the disc.

2. You cannot move your feet once you are in possession of the disc, and you have just ten seconds to pass, so think quickly. Remember, you are aiming to get the disc to a team-mate who is within your opponents' end zone to score a point.

3. Each time a point is scored, the teams must line up in front of their end zones again to restart play. The team that has just scored is the offence team, so the other team must pass the disc to them.

4. Ultimate is a non-contact sport, so if you bump into another player it is a foul. If the player loses the disc to your team because of your foul, it must be given back.

5. If your team-mate does not catch your pass, or if he catches your pass, but isn't in bounds, with his feet within the field of play, the disc must be given to the other team.

Once one of the teams gets to 10 points, take a 10-minute break. The winning team are the first to reach 19 points if they are at least two points clear of their opponents. Otherwise, the first team to reach 21 points are the 'ultimate' winners.

DISC DEXTERITY

The disc can be thrown in lots of different ways, but all throws require good timing and a supple wrist action. Practise with a throwing partner to perfect your technique. For each of the throws here, grip the disc with your fingers underneath and thumb on top. The disc should be level with your arm. Release the disc as your arm swings around in line with your throwing partner. Here's how to achieve some point-scoring moves.

The backhand. This is the most common, and most powerful, throw. Stand at a slight angle to the person you are aiming at. Bring your arm across your body then swing it forwards, flicking your wrist through as you release the disc. If the disc is tilted to one side as it leaves your hand it will curve in the air.

The forehand. This is a speedy throw, used when you haven't got the time or space to wind up a backhand. Quickly bring your arm out to the side and release the disc with a strong wrist flick.

The hammer. Finally there's a special Ultimate throw known as the 'hammer', which is similar to a tennis serve. Take your arm back over your head and flick the disc forwards with a smooth motion, keeping your arm vertical as it passes your head – perfect when someone is blocking you. The disc will fly high and in a huge curve like a boomerang.

HOW TO MAKE THE MOST OF YOUR LAP OF HONOUR

Years of hard training have finally paid off – the crowd are on their feet and the sound of their cheering is almost deafening, but what should you do? Whether you're in a football stadium or an athletics arena, your winning moment in front of the crowd will be over in just minutes. Take advantage of this time to bask in all the glory and take a lap of honour.

AND THE CROWD GOES WILD

• Do kneel down and kiss the track, or the grass – don't worry about hygiene – the idea is to show how grateful you are to the wonderful arena you have competed in.

• Do remember to trot over to your fans – lots of people

have come especially to see you – and then you can ask for a flag, or your club's scarf, so that you can hold it over your head for the photographers. This will make a great shot to look back on, and these images will last forever.•
Do walk or run around the stadium, applauding the crowd until your arms ache too much to clap any more. After all, their cheering and support has contributed to a great atmosphere that helped you win.

• Do punch the air, jump up and down, wave and smile until your face hurts – this is no time for shyness.

• If you have won a race, remember to shake hands with your opponents – if you are part of a team, high-five your team-mates every chance you get.

• Relax and begin to enjoy the focus of the world's attention. You really are unbeatable.

UNBEATABLE GLOSSARY

This is a list of sporting words and their explanations for you to refer to. Any words shown in *italics* are explained in a separate entry.

Addressing: positioning yourself so that you are facing towards the ball or target

Back foot: the foot furthest from your target when you are standing side-on to it

Ball: in baseball, when the ball is pitched outside of the *strike zone* – four 'balls' and the batter takes a free 'walk' to first base

Bounds (in and out of): a player or ball that is either in or out of the boundary of the playing field

Bowler: in cricket, the person who throws the ball towards the batsman

Defence: the players on your team, when the opposing team has the ball, defending your goal or scoring area

Discipline: a specific sport or skill within a sport

Drill: a practice exercise to improve a particular skill

Fielder and outfielder: in cricket/ baseball, when the opposing team bats, a person who tries to catch the ball when it has been hit. In cricket the outfield is the area furthest from the stumps, but in baseball the outfield is the area outside of the four bases

Follow through: continuing to move your arm or hand in the direction of the target after you have thrown or hit the ball

Foul: a play against a member of the opposing team that is against the rules

Front foot: the foot nearest your target when you are standing side-on to it

Grounding: in rugby, placing the ball on the ground on the other side of the goal line

Marking: in team sports, staying close to a member of the opposing team to try to stop them getting or passing the ball

Momentum: a build up of power, when cycling or running for example, that causes less effort to be needed to maintain that speed

Mount and dismount: getting on or off a piece of sporting equipment, a bicycle for example

Offence: the players on your team, when your team has the ball, attacking the opposing team's goal or scoring area

Pitcher: in baseball, the person who throws the ball

Slipstream: the flow of air behind a fast-moving competitor, which protects you from a head-on breeze and sometimes allows you to reduce the effort you need to make to move forward

Spin: adding extra rotation when you hit or throw a ball, by hitting it off-centre or adding a slight twist of the wrist as you launch it

Sponsors: a company or person who gives funding to a sports-person in exchange for displaying their logo and promoting their products

Stamina: being able to keep up energy and strength for a sustained length of time

Stance: when standing ready to play, in golf or baseball for example, with the correct posture to hit the ball

Streamlined: positioning your body in a smooth shape so that you get maximum speed and less resistance in air or water

Stride: a regular pace, when running for instance

Strike: in ten-pin bowling, knocking down all ten pins at once – in baseball, when a batter misses a pitch that is within the *strike zone*, see *ball*

Strike out: in baseball, three missed pitches, meaning that the batter is out

Strike zone: in baseball, the area roughly between the batter's knee and chest to which the *pitcher* must throw the ball

Strong hand: the hand that you are naturally comfortable using (usually the hand you write with)

Tee: in golf, a wooden or plastic peg to hold up the ball – in rugby, a plastic disc or mound of earth on which to rest the ball

Time trial: in cycling for example, competing separately to get the best time over a set course

Trajectory: the curved path of a moving ball or object

Weak hand: the hand you are less comfortable using, usually weaker than your strong hand

ALSO AVAILABLE ...

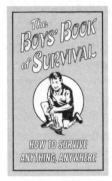

The Boys' Book Of Survival:
How To Survive
Anything, Anywhere

ISBN: 978-1-906082-12-3

The Boys' Book Of Spycraft:
How To Be The Best
Secret Agent Ever

ISBN: 978-1-906082-39-0

The Boys' Book 1:
How To Be The Best
At Everything

ISBN: 978-1-905158-64-5

The Boys' Book 2:
How To Be The Best
At Everything Again

ISBN: 978-1-906082-33-8

The Boys' Book 3:
Even More Ways To Be
The Best At Everything

ISBN: 978-1-906082-75-8